ISSUE ONE
COVER A
MIKE S. MILLER

ISSUE ONE
COVER B

MICHAEL KALUTA

George R. R. Martin's The Hedge Knight
The Graphic Novel

WRITTEN BY
GEORGE R. R. MARTIN

ADAPTATION BY
BEN AVERY

PENCILS BY
MIKE S. MILLER

COLORS BY
MIKE CROWELL

COLORS BY
TEAM KANDORA
TRANSPARENCY DIGITAL

LETTERED BY
BILL TORTOLINI
LITHIUM PRO DESIGN

COVER ART BY
MIKE S. MILLER

COVER COLORED BY
MOHAN SIVAKAMI

EDITED BY
ROBERT SILVERBERG

THEMATIC CONSULTANTS
ELIO M. GARCIA &
LINDA ANTONSSON

JET CITY COMICS EDITION DESIGN BY
DERON BENNETT
ANDWORLD DESIGN

SENIOR PRODUCTION MANAGER
JILL TAPLIN

SENIOR COLLECTION EDITOR
ALEX CARR

Published by Jet City Comics, Seattle www.apub.com
Library of Congress Catalog Number: 2013914372
ISBN-13: 9781477849101 ISBN-10: 1477849106 EISBN: 9781477899106

HE HAD A LONG LIFE. CLOSER TO SIXTY THAN TO FIFTY.
HOW MANY MEN CAN SAY THAT? STILL...

I THOUGHT IT WOULD BE DIFFERENT.
SER ARLAN DIED THE WAY HE LIVED - AS A HEDGE KNIGHT.
RIDING FROM KEEP TO KEEP.
TAKING SERVICE WITH THIS LORD AND THAT LORD.
FIGHTING IN THEIR BATTLES--
--AND EATING IN THEIR HALLS UNTIL THE WAR WAS DONE.
THEN MOVING ON.
THERE WERE TOURNEYS FROM TIME TO TIME AS WELL.

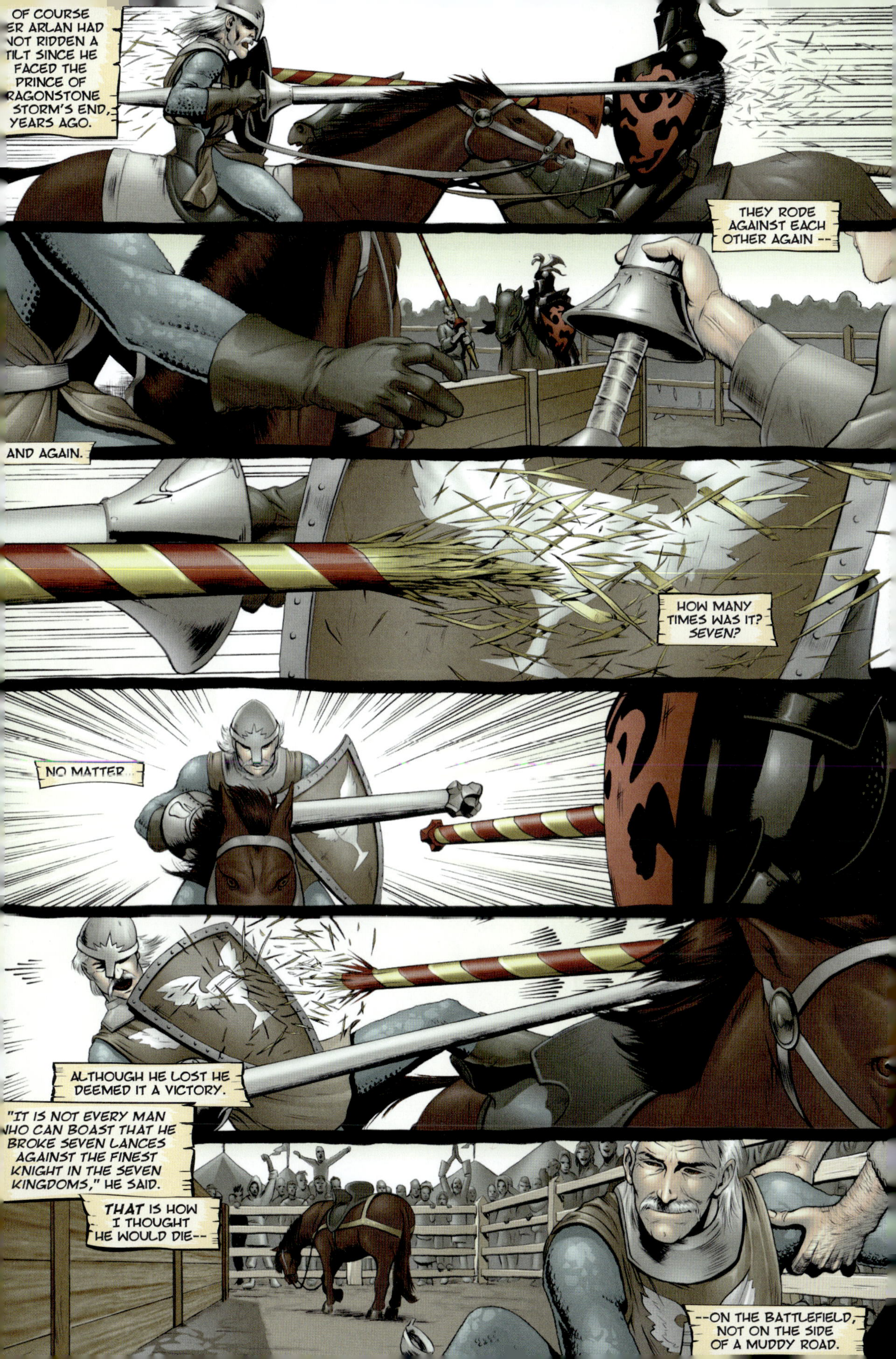
OF COURSE ER ARLAN HAD NOT RIDDEN A TILT SINCE HE FACED THE PRINCE OF RAGONSTONE STORM'S END, YEARS AGO.
THEY RODE AGAINST EACH OTHER AGAIN --
AND AGAIN.
HOW MANY TIMES WAS IT? SEVEN?
NO MATTER...
ALTHOUGH HE LOST HE DEEMED IT A VICTORY.
"IT IS NOT EVERY MAN HO CAN BOAST THAT HE BROKE SEVEN LANCES AGAINST THE FINEST KNIGHT IN THE SEVEN KINGDOMS," HE SAID.
THAT IS HOW I THOUGHT HE WOULD DIE--
--ON THE BATTLEFIELD, NOT ON THE SIDE OF A MUDDY ROAD.

BUT SER ARLAN USED TO WATCH THE SUNSET AND SAY TO ME, "ANOTHER DAY DONE AND WHO KNOWS WHAT THE MORROW WILL BRING US, EH, DUNK?"
WELL, ONE MORROW BROUGHT THE RAINS. THE ONE AFTER HAD BROUGHT WET GUSTY WINDS. AND THE NEXT A CHILL.
THE FOURTH DAY THE OLD MAN WAS TOO WEAK TO RIDE.
AND NOW HE WAS GONE.
BURIED IN A PATHETIC GRAVE WITHOUT EVEN A SEPTON TO SAY SOME PRAYERS OVER HIM.
ONLY ME.
I'D LEAVE YOUR SWORD, BUT IT WOULD RUST IN THE GROUND.
THE GODS WILL GIVE YOU A NEW ONE, I GUESS.
I WISH YOU DIDN'T DIE, SER.
YOU WERE A TRUE KNIGHT AND YOU NEVER BEAT ME WHEN I DIDN'T DESERVE IT ...
... EXCEPT THAT ONE TIME IN MAIDENPOOL.
IT WAS THE INN BOY WHO ATE THE WIDOW WOMAN'S PIE, NOT ME, I TOLD YOU. IT DON'T MATTER NOW.
THE GODS KEEP YOU, SER.

WHAT NOW, SWEETFOOT?
IF I SOLD THUNDER AND OLD CHESTNUT, AND THE SADDLES AND THE BRIDLES TOO, I'D COME AWAY WITH ENOUGH SILVER TO--
NO.
THE LIFE OF A HEDGE KNIGHT IS THE ONLY LIFE I KNOW.
I COULD FIND ANOTHER HEDGE KNIGHT IN NEED OF A SQUIRE TO TEND HIS ANIMALS AND CLEAN HIS MAIL.
OR I COULD GO TO SOME CITY -- TO LANNISPORT OR KING'S LANDING -- AND JOIN THEIR CITY GUARD.
OR...

IT FITS MY GRIP AS WELL AS IT EVER FIT HIS.
AND THERE IS A TOURNEY AT ASHFORD MEADOW...

THE OLD MAN LEFT THREE SILVER STAGS -- ENOUGH FOR A GOOD MEAL AND ENOUGH ALE AS I CARED TO DRINK -- AND NINETEEN COPPER PENNIES.
THE WARM YELLOW LIGHT SPILLING FROM THE INN'S WINDOWS WAS INVITING, BUT I HAD TO BE CAREFUL WITH MY COIN.
WHILE I WOULD HAVE LIKED NOTHING BETTER AFTER A GOOD WARM MEAL THAN A SOFT STRAW MATTRESS AND A ROOF ABOVE MY HEAD, THE GROUND WOULD SERVE TONIGHT.
ARE YOU THE STABLEBOY?
I'LL WANT MY PALFREY RUBBED DOWN. AND OATS FOR ALL THREE. CAN YOU TEND TO THEM?
I COULD.
IF I WANTED.
I'LL HAVE NONE OF THAT. I AM A KNIGHT, I'LL HAVE YOU KNOW.
YOU DON'T LOOK TO BE A KNIGHT.
DO ALL KNIGHTS LOOK THE SAME?
NO, BUT THEY DON'T LOOK LIKE YOU, EITHER. YOUR SWORD BELT IS MADE OF ROPE.
SO LONG AS IT HOLDS MY SCABBARD, IT SERVES.
SEE TO MY HORSES. YOU'LL GET A COPPER IF YOU DO WELL AND A CLOUT IN THE EAR IF YOU DON'T.

SIT WHERE YOU LIKE!
IS IT ALE YOU WANT OR FOOD?
BOTH!
THERE'S GOOD LAMB, ROASTED WITH A CRUST OF HERBS, AND SOME DUCKS MY SON SHOT DOWN.
WHICH WILL YOU HAVE?
BOTH!
WELL, YOU'RE BIG ENOUGH FOR IT.
WILL YOU BE WANTING A ROOM AS WELL?
NO, SOME FOOD, SOME ALE, AND IT'S ON TO ASHFORD FOR ME.
HOW MUCH FARTHER IS IT?
A DAY'S RIDE.
IS MY BOY SEEING TO YOUR HORSES OR HAS HE RUN OFF AGAIN?
NO, HE'S THERE.
YOU SEEM TO HAVE NO CUSTOM.
HALF THE TOWN'S GONE TO THE TOURNEY.
MY OWN WOULD AS WELL, IF I ALLOWED IT.
THE BOY WOULD RATHER SWAGGER ABOUT WITH SOLDIERS, AND THE GIRL TURNS TO SIGHS AND GIGGLES EVERY TIME A KNIGHT RIDES BY.
COULDN'T TELL YOU WHY.. KNIGHTS ARE BUILT THE SAM AS OTHER MEN, AND I NEVE KNEW A JOUST TO CHANG THE PRICE OF EGGS.
YOU'RE BOUND FOR THE TOURNEY YOURSELF?

AYE.
I MEAN TO BE A CHAMPION.
DO YOU, NOW?
YOU!

I DREAMED OF YOU.
YOU STAY AWAY FROM ME, YOU HEAR?
YOU STAY WELL AWAY!
MY LORD?
NEVER YOU MIND THAT ONE, SER.
ALL HE DOES IS DRINK AND TALK ABOUT HIS DREAMS.
I'LL SEE ABOUT THAT FOOD.
FOOD?
I'M GOING TO BE SICK.
I WANTED A WHORE, BUT THERE'S NONE TO BE FOUND.
ALL GONE TO ASHFORD MEADOW.
GODS BE GOOD, I NEED SOME WINE...

THE LAMB WAS AS GOOD AS ANY I HAVE EATEN--
--AND THE DUCK WAS EVEN BETTER.
I HAD A SECOND TANKARD OF ALE WITH THE MEAL, A THIRD TO WASH IT ALL DOWN, AND A FOURTH BECAUSE THERE WAS NO ONE TO TELL ME I COULDN'T.
I PAID THE WOMAN WITH A SILVER AND STILL GOT BACK A HANDFUL OF COPPERS.
THIS IS WHAT IT MEANT TO BE A KNIGHT.
GOOD FOOD, ALE WHENEVER I WANTED IT, AND NO ONE TO CLOUT ME ON THE HEAD.
NEEEIGH
EASY, LAD.
WHAT?
WHAT'S GOING--

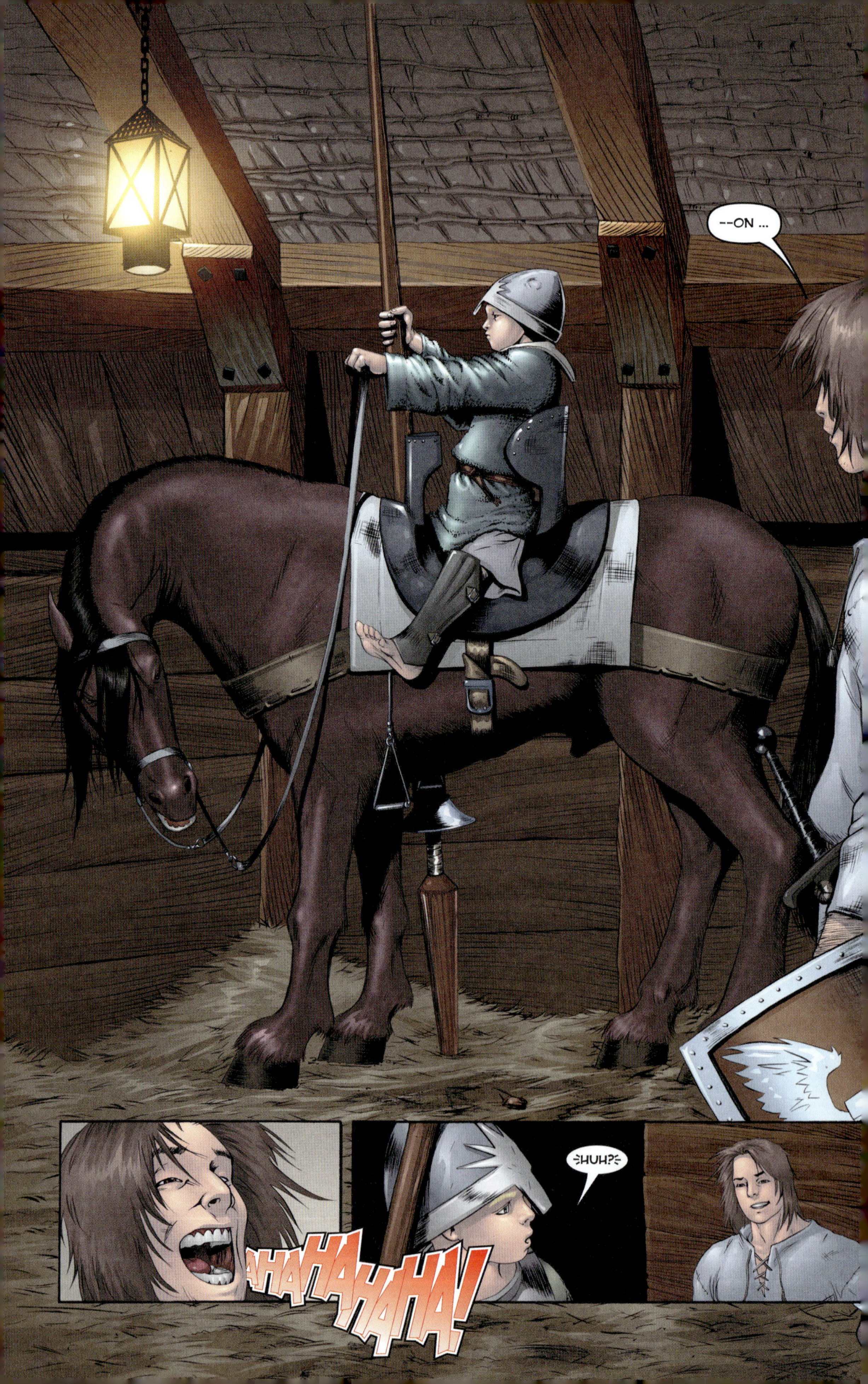
--ON ...
HAHAHAHAHA!
HUH?

MY LORD, I DID NOT MEAN--
THIEF.
TAKE OFF THAT ARMOR, AND BE GLAD THUNDER DIDN'T KICK YOU IN THAT FOOL HEAD.
HE'S A WARHORSE, NOT A BOY'S PONY.
I COULD RIDE HIM AS WELL AS YOU.
OSE YOUR OUTH-- I'LL AVE NONE OF YOUR NSOLENCE.
THE HAUBERK TOO, TAKE IT OFF.
WHAT DO YOU THINK YOU WERE DOING?
HOW CAN I TELL YOU WITH MY MOUTH CLOSED?
YOU CAN OPEN YOUR MOUTH TO ANSWER.
NOW PICK UP THAT MAIL, SHAKE OFF THE DIRT, AND PUT IT BACK WHERE YOU FOUND IT.
AND THE HALFHELM TOO.
DID YOU FEED THE HORSES AND RUB DOWN SWEETFOOT AS I TOLD YOU?
YES.
YOU'RE GOING TO ASHFORD, AREN'T YOU?
TAKE ME WITH YOU, SER.

THE INNKEEPER HAD WARNED ME OF THIS.
AND WHAT MIGHT YOUR MOTHER SAY TO THAT?
MY MOTHER? MY MOTHER'S DEAD, SHE WOULDN'T SAY ANYTHING.
WHAT ABOUT--
IT DIDN'T MAKE SENS BUT MY HEAD WAS STILL A LITTLE FUZZ FROM THE ALE. PERHAPS HE WAS ONC APPRENTICED TO THE INNKEEP.
ARE YOU AN ORPHAN BOY?
ARE YOU?
I WAS. ONCE.
TILL THE OLD MAN TOOK ME IN.
IF YOU TOOK ME, I COULD SQUIRE FOR YOU.
I HAVE NO NEED FOR A SQUIRE.
EVERY KNIGHT NEEDS A SQUIRE.
YOU LOOK LIKE YOU NEED ONE MORE THAN MOST.
AND YOU LOOK LIKE YOU NEED A CLOUT IN THE EAR!
FILL ME A SACK OF OATS.
I'M OFF TO ASHFORD--
--ALONE.

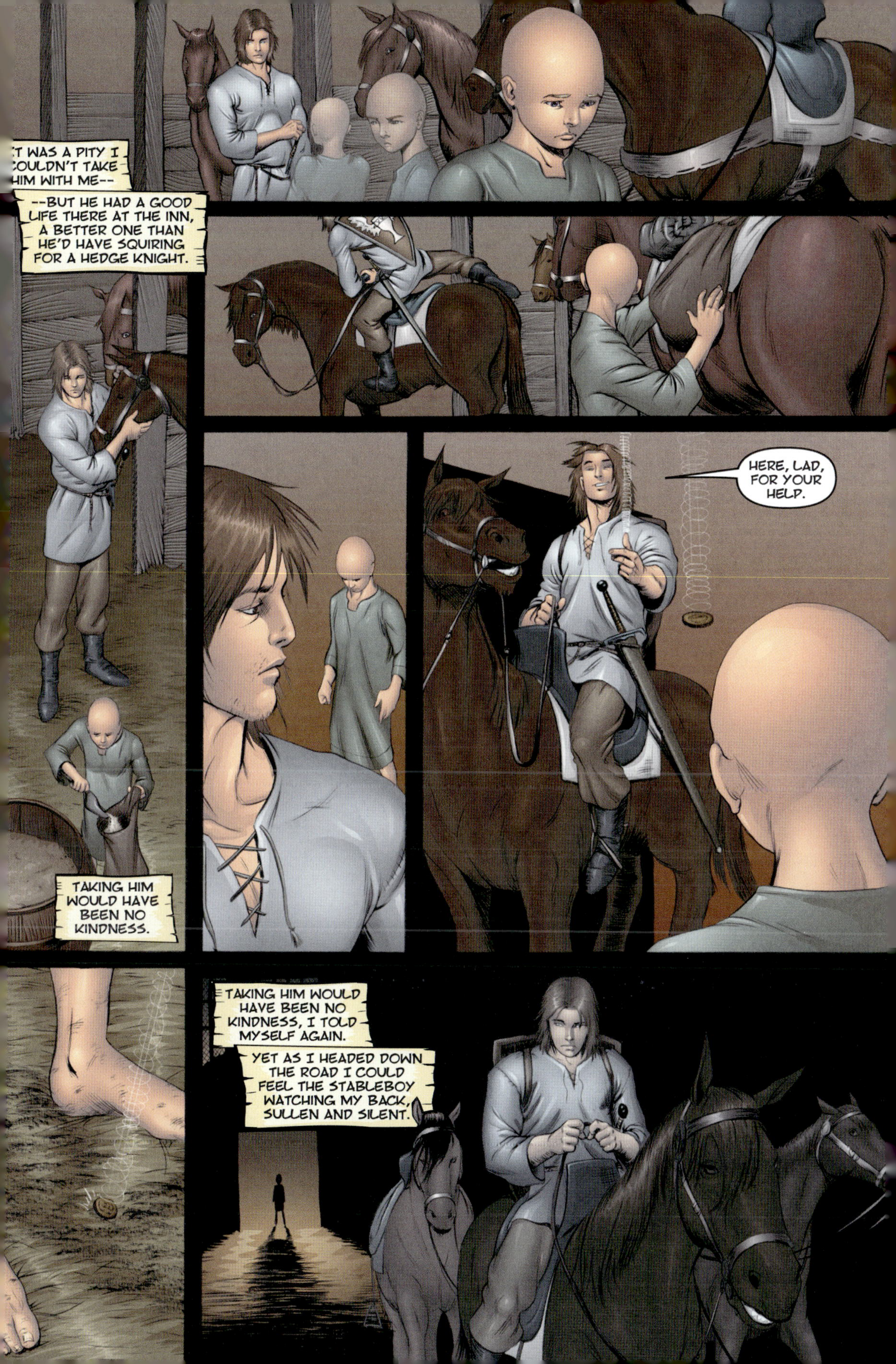
IT WAS A PITY I COULDN'T TAKE HIM WITH ME--
--BUT HE HAD A GOOD LIFE THERE AT THE INN, A BETTER ONE THAN HE'D HAVE SQUIRING FOR A HEDGE KNIGHT.
TAKING HIM WOULD HAVE BEEN NO KINDNESS.
HERE, LAD, FOR YOUR HELP.
TAKING HIM WOULD HAVE BEEN NO KINDNESS, I TOLD MYSELF AGAIN.
YET AS I HEADED DOWN THE ROAD I COULD FEEL THE STABLEBOY WATCHING MY BACK, SULLEN AND SILENT.

ASHFORD MEADOW.
THE OLD MAN HAD RIDDEN WITH SOME OF THESE KNIGHTS; OTHERS I KNEW FROM TALES TOLD IN COMMON ROOMS AND ROUND CAMPFIRES.
I'D NEVER LEARNED THE MAGIC OF READING AND WRITING, BUT THE OLD MA HAD BEEN RELENTLESS WHEN IT CAME TO TEACHING ME HERALDRY.
A THREADBARE WOOL CLOAK WOULD BE MY SHELTER THAT NIGHT.
MY SUPPER WOULD BE A HARD, STRINGY PIECE OF SALT BEEF.
IF I MADE MY CA UPON THAT GAUD FIELD, I WOULD SUFFER BOTH SILENT SCORN AN OPEN MOCKERY
A FEW WOULD PERHAPS TREAT M KINDLY, YET IN WAY THAT WAS ALMOST WORSE

THE NIGHTINGALES OF LORD CARON OF THE MARCHES. THE CROWNED STAG FOR SER LYONEL BARATHEON, THE LAUGHING STORM. THE TARLY HUNTSMAN. HOUSE DONDARRION'S PURPLE LIGHTNING. THE RED APPLE OF THE FOSSOWAYS.
LANNISTER, PENROSE, MARBRAND, HIGHTOWER, FREY...
IT SEEMED AS THOUGH EVERY LORDLY HOUSE OF THE WEST AND SOUTH HAD SENT A KNIGHT OR THREE TO SEE THE FAIR MAID AND BRAVE THE LISTS IN HER HONOR.
A HEDGE KNIGHT MUST HOLD TIGHT TO HIS PRIDE.
I MUST EARN MY PLACE IN THAT COMPANY.
IF I FOUGHT WELL, SOME LORD MAY TAKE ME INTO HIS HOUSEHOLD.
THEN, FRESH MEAT EVERY NIGHT IN A CASTLE HALL AND MY OWN PAVILION AT TOURNEYS.
BUT FIRST I MUST DO WELL.

ON THE OUTSKIRTS OF THE GREAT MEADOW A GOOD HALF MILE FROM TOWN AND CASTLE I FOUND A PLACE WHERE A BEND IN THE BROOK HAD FORMED A DEEP POOL.
IT WAS A PRETTY SPOT, AND NO ONE HAD LAID CLAIM TO IT.
THIS WOULD BE MY PAVILION, A PAVILION ROOFED WITH LEAVES, GREENER EVEN THAN THE BANNERS OF THE TYRELLS AND THE ESTERMONTS.
IT HAD BEEN A LONG DAY. I WAS COVERED IN THE DUST OF TRAVEL.
HE INSISTED THAT WE WASH OURSELVES HEAD TO HEELS EVERY TIME THE MOON TURNED, WHETHER WE SMELLED SOUR OR NOT.
NOW THAT I WAS A KNIGHT, *I* VOWED TO DO THE SAME.
AFTERWARD, I SAT UNDER THE ELM AND LET THE WARM SPRING AIR DRY MY SKIN AND WATCHED A DRAGONFLY MOVE LAZILY AMONG THE REEDS.
I WONDERED WHY THEY WOULD NAME IT A DRAGONFLY -- IT LOOKED NOTHING LIKE A DRAGON.
NOT THAT I HAD EVER SEEN A DRAGON.
BUT THE OLD MAN HAD.

I'D HEARD THE STORY HALF A HUNDRED TIMES.
HE'D SAY:
I WAS JUST A LITTLE BOY, AND MY GRANDFATHER TOOK ME TO KING'S LANDING.
WHILE WE WERE THERE, I SAW THE LAST DRAGON.
"IT WAS THE YEAR BEFORE IT DIED. SHE WAS A GREEN FEMALE -- SMALL AND STUNTED -- HER WINGS WITHERED.
"NONE OF HER EGGS EVER HATCHED.
"SOME SAY KING AEGON POISONED HER -- THE THIRD AEGON, THAT WOULD BE, THE ONE THEY NAMED DRAGONBANE.
"AEGON THE UNLUCKY."
TELL ME 'BOUT THE DRAGON, SER.
AGAIN?
"HE WAS AFRAID OF DRAGONS, FOR HE'D SEEN HIS UNCLE'S BEAST DEVOUR HIS OWN MOTHER.
"THE SUMMERS HAVE BEEN SHORTER SINCE THE LAST DRAGON DIED, AND THE WINTERS LONGER AND CRUELER."

AND THE DRAGON RAISED ITS HEAD AND ROARED!
ROAAAARRRRRR
ALONG THE EDGE OF THE FIELD, DOZENS OF MERCHANTS HAD ERECTED THEIR STALLS.
DIE, BEAST
HAVE AT THEE!
SELLING FELTS AND FRUITS, BELTS AND BOOTS, HIDES AND HAWKS, GEMSTONES, SPICES, FOOD, ALL MANNER OF GOODS.
I WATCHED A PUPPET KNIGHT BATTLE A PUPPET DRAGON WHILE I ATE.
THE PUPPETS WERE GOOD -- SKILLFULLY CRAFTED AND MANIPULATED.
ALTHOUGH, TRUTH BE TOLD, I THINK I WATCHED THE PUPPETEER MORE THAN THE PUPPETS.
I WOULD HAVE TOSSED THE GI A COPPER IF I' HAD ONE TO SPARE, BUT JU NOW I NEEDE EVERY COIN.
FOR ON THE MORROW I WOULD ENROLL MY NAME ON THE LISTS --
-- BUT I HAD OTHER MATTER TO LOOK INTO THIS NIGHT IF HOPED TO CHALLENGE.

I NEED ARMOR FOR THE TOURNEY.
A SUIT OF GOOD MAIL, WITH GORGET, GREAVES, AND GREATHELM.
YOU DO GOOD WORK.
NONE BETTER.
YOU'RE A BIG ONE, BUT I'VE ARMORED BIGGER.
KNEEL, I WANT TO MEASURE THOSE SHOULDERS AND THAT NECK OF YOURS.
HMM.
LIFT YOUR ARM.
HUHNH.
YOU CAN STAND.
UH-HUH.
I HAVE SOME PIECES IN ME WAGON THAT MIGHT DO FOR YOU.
NOTHING PRETTIED UP WITH GOLD OR SILVER, MIND YOU, JUST GOOD STEEL, STRONG AND PLAIN.
I MAKE HELMS THAT LOOK LIKE HELMS, NOT WINGED PIGS AND QUEER FOREIGN FRUITS, BUT MINE'LL SERVE YOU BETTER IF YOU TAKE A LANCE IN THE FACE.
THAT'S ALL I WANT. HOW MUCH?
EIGHT HUNDRED STAGS, FOR I'M FEELING KINDLY.
EIGHT... HUNDRED?

I... I COULD TRADE YOU SOME OLD ARMOR...
...MADE FOR A SMALLER MAN... A HALFHELM, A MAIL HAUBERK..
STEELY PATE SELLS ONLY HIS OWN WORK.
BUT--
BUT IT MIGHT BE I COULD MAKE USE OF THE METAL.
IF IT'S NOT TOO RUSTED, I'LL TAKE IT AND ARMOR YOU FOR SIX HUNDRED.
I'LL GIVE YOU TWO SILVERS NOW, AND THE ARMOR AND THE REST OF THE COIN ON THE MORROW.
TWO SILVERS BUYS YOU A DAY.
AFTER THAT, I SELL ME WORK TO THE NEXT MAN.
YOU'LL GET IT ALL--
--I MEAN TO BE A CHAMPION HERE.
DO YOU?
AND THESE OTHER KNIGHTS, I SUPPOSE THEY ALL CAME JUST TO CHEER YOU ON?

ONE VICTORY IS ALL I NEED.
THAT'S NOT SO MUCH TO HOPE FOR.
EVEN SO, THE OLD MAN WOULD NEVER HAVE HOPED FOR IT.
"IT IS NOT EVERY MAN WHO CAN BOAST THAT HE BROKE SEVEN LANCES AGAINST THE FINEST KNIGHT IN THE SEVEN KINGDOMS," HE SAID.
BUT IT DIDN'T STOP THERE. "I COULD NEVER HOPE TO DO BETTER, SO WHY SHOULD I TRY."
AND HE NEVER RODE TILT AGAIN.
WHAT IS THIS?
BUT I WAS QUICK AND I WAS STRONG, HE ALWAYS SAID SO, WHAT WAS TRUE FOR HIM NEED NOT BE TRUE FOR ME.
MY ARMOR...
THE HORSES...
LEAVE MY HORSES ALONE, SONS OF...
HUH?

YOU!
WHAT ARE YOU DOING HERE?
COOKING A FISH.
DO YOU WANT SOME?

ISSUE TWO
COVER A
MIKE S. MILLER

ISSUE TWO
COVER B

Tom Mandrake

HIS WAS THE LAST FACE I EXPECTED.
HOW DID YOU GET HERE?
I RODE IN THE BACK OF A CART WITH A MAN DELIVERING LAMBS TO ASHFORD CASTLE.
WELL, YOU'D BETTER FIND ANOTHER CART.
YOU CAN'T MAKE ME GO!
I'VE HAD ENOUGH OF THAT INN.
AND I'VE HAD ENOUGH OF YOUR INSOLENCE!
I SHOULD THROW YOU OVER MY HORSE RIGHT NOW AND TAKE YOU HOME--
YOU'D MISS THE TOURNEY--YOU'D NEED TO RIDE ALL THE WAY TO KING'S LANDING!
KING'S LANDING?
FOR A MOMENT I THOUGHT HE MOCKED ME, BUT HE COULD NOT HAVE KNOWN I HAD BEEN BORN IN KING'S LANDING AS WELL.
ANOTHER WRETCH FROM FLEA BOTTOM. WHO COULD BLAME HIM FOR WANTING OUT OF THAT PLACE?
WHAT ARE THOSE DOING THERE?
I WASHED THEM. AND GROOMED THE HORSES AND MADE THE FIRE AND CAUGHT THIS FISH.
I WOULD HAVE RAISED YOUR PAVILION, BUT I COULDN'T FIND ONE.

SO THEY DO!
TRUTH IS, I LACK THE COIN FOR A PAVILION.
YOU'D BEST TURN THIS FISH -- IT'LL BURN ON THE BOTTOM AND BE RAW ON TOP.
YOU'D NEVER MAKE A KITCHEN BOY.
I WOULD IF I WANTED.
WHAT HAPPENED TO YOUR HAIR, BOY?
THE MAESTERS SHAVED IT.
WHY? ARE YOU ILL? YOU HAVE LICE?
THERE'S ALL THE PAVILION A TRUE KNIGHT NEEDS.
WHAT IF IT RAINS?
THE TREE WILL SHELTER ME.
TREES LEAK.
NO, SER..
WHAT'S YOUR NAME?
DUNK.
DUNK?
SER DUNK?
THAT'S NO NAME FOR A KNIGHT!
IS IT SHORT FOR DUNCAN?
DUNCAN? THE OLD MAN JUST CALLED ME DUNK AS LONG AS I COULD RECALL...

DUNCAN, YES, SER DUNCAN OF...
OF WHAT? FLEA BOTTOM?
SER DUNCAN THE TALL.
NEVER HEARD OF YOU.
AND YOU KNOW EVERY KNIGHT IN THE SEVEN KINGDOMS?
THE GOOD ONES.
DO YOU HAVE A NAME, THIEF?
YES... EGG.
I SHOULD BEAT YOU AND SEND YOU ON YOUR WAY, EGG, BUT--
I HAVE NO SQUIRE.
IF YOU DO AS YOU'RE TOLD, YOU CAN SERVE ME FOR THE TOURNEY.
AFTER THAT, WE'LL SEE.
YES, MY LORD.
SER. I AM ONLY A HEDGE KNIGHT.
YES, SER.
NOW, LET'S TRY SOME OF THAT FISH...
SEE IF YOU REALLY COULD BE A KITCHEN BOY...

THE FISH WAS A LITTLE RAW, AND HE HAD NOT REMOVED ALL THE BONES, BUT IT TASTED A WORLD BETTER THAN HARD SALT BEEF.
THE BOY WAS ASLEEP NOT LONG AFTER THAT.
HE SEEMED A LIKELY YOUNG LAD, MIGHT ONE DAY MAKE A KNIGHT.
AND I COULD TEACH HIM, SAME AS ARLAN TAUGHT ME.
A HALF MILE AWAY I HEARD THE MUSIC FROM THE TOURNEY GROUND.
BUT WHAT I SAW ABOVE...
IT'S SAID A FALLING STAR BRINGS LUCK TO THOSE WHO SEE IT.
THE REST OF THEM WERE ALL IN THEIR PAVILIONS BY NOW, STARING UP AT SILK INSTEAD OF SKY.
SO THE LUCK WAS ALL MINE.

UP.
THERE'S WORK TO DO.
WHAT ABOUT BREAKFAST?
THERE'S SALT BEEF. AFTER WE'RE DONE.
I'D SOONER EAT THE HORSE... SER.
YOU'LL EAT MY FIST IF YOU DON'T DO AS YOU'RE TOLD.
I EXPECT I'LL BE GONE MOST OF THE DAY.
YOU'RE TO STAY HERE AND PUT THE CAMP IN ORDER AND MAKE SURE NO OTHER THIEVES COME NOSING ABOUT.
AND YOU HAD BETTER BE HERE WHEN I GET BACK.
ROB ME AND I WILL HUNT YOU DOWN.
WITH DOGS.
YOU DON'T HAVE ANY DOGS.
I'LL GET SOME.
JUST FOR YOU.

THE WHITEWASHED HOUSES OF THE MARKET TOWN SURROUNDING ASHFORD CASTLE HAD AN INVITING ASPECT TO THEM.
WHEN I WAS YOUNGER, I USED TO WONDER WHAT IT'D BE LIKE TO LIVE IN SUCH A PLACE...
A ROOF OVER YOUR HEAD EVERY NIGHT AND WAKING EVERY MORNING WITH THE SAME WALLS WRAPPED AROUND YOU.
ARE YOU PLUMMER THE STEWARD?
WHAT DO YOU WANT?
IF I DID WELL HERE, I COULD SOON KNOW WHAT IT WAS LIKE -- AND EGG TOO -- STRANGER THINGS HAPPENED EVERY DAY.
I CAME FOR THE TOURNEY. TO ENTER THE LISTS.
MY LORD'S TOURNEY IS A CONTEST FOR KNIGHTS.
ARE YOU A KNIGHT?
YES.
A KNIGHT WITH A NAME, MAYHAPS?
OH... YES.
ER, SER DUNCAN.
THE, UH, TALL.
AND WHERE MIGHT YOU BE FROM, "SER DUNCAN THE TALL"?
EVERYPLACE. I WAS SQUIRE TO SER ARLAN OF PENNYTREE SINCE I WAS FIVE OR SIX...
THIS IS HIS SHIELD...
HE WAS COMING HERE, BUT HE CAUGHT A CHILL AND DIED, SO I CAME IN HIS STEAD.

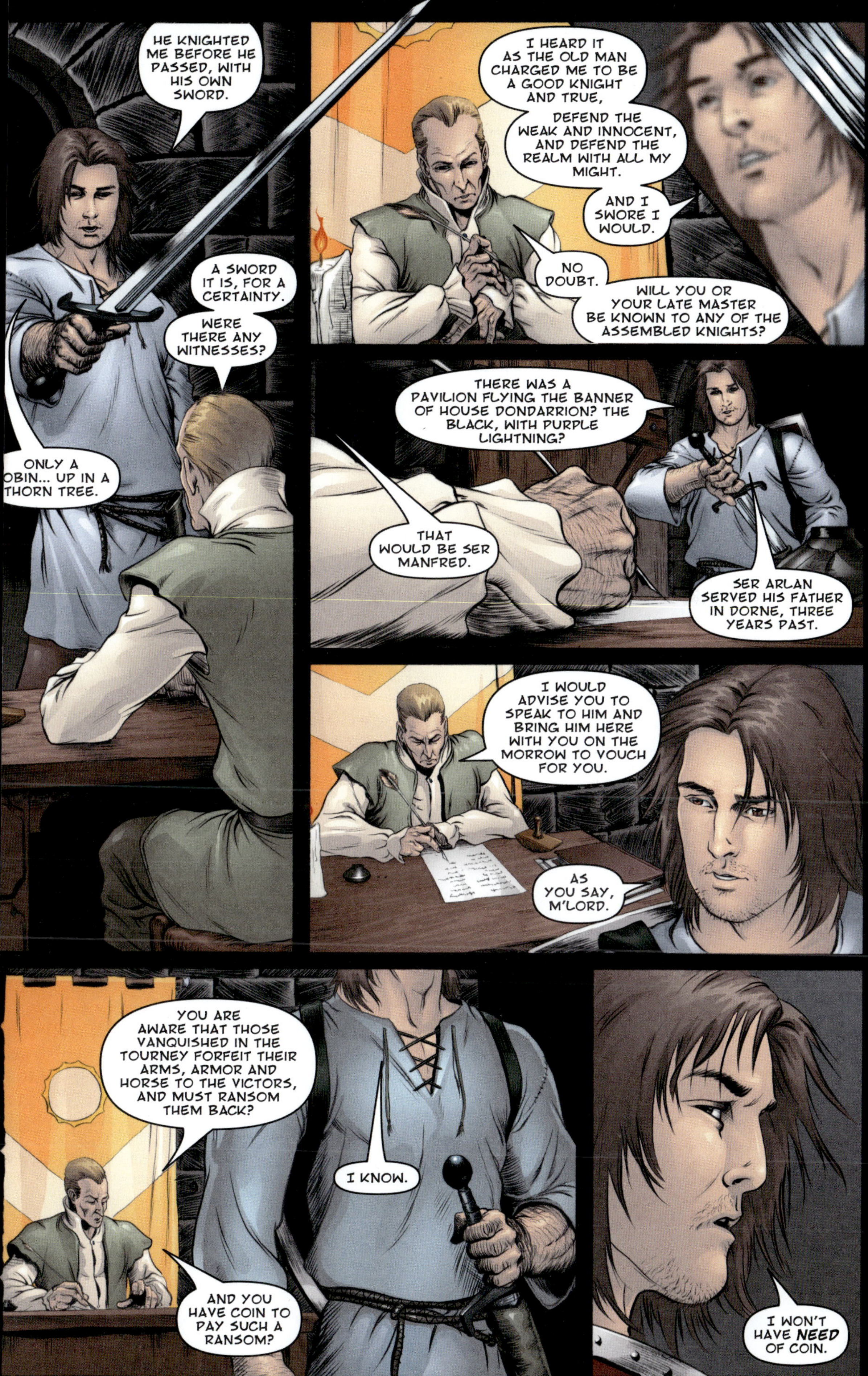
HE KNIGHTED ME BEFORE HE PASSED, WITH HIS OWN SWORD.
A SWORD IT IS, FOR A CERTAINTY.
WERE THERE ANY WITNESSES?
ONLY A OBIN... UP IN A THORN TREE.
I HEARD IT AS THE OLD MAN CHARGED ME TO BE A GOOD KNIGHT AND TRUE,
DEFEND THE WEAK AND INNOCENT, AND DEFEND THE REALM WITH ALL MY MIGHT.
AND I SWORE I WOULD.
NO DOUBT.
WILL YOU OR YOUR LATE MASTER BE KNOWN TO ANY OF THE ASSEMBLED KNIGHTS?
THERE WAS A PAVILION FLYING THE BANNER OF HOUSE DONDARRION? THE BLACK, WITH PURPLE LIGHTNING?
THAT WOULD BE SER MANFRED.
SER ARLAN SERVED HIS FATHER IN DORNE, THREE YEARS PAST.
I WOULD ADVISE YOU TO SPEAK TO HIM AND BRING HIM HERE WITH YOU ON THE MORROW TO VOUCH FOR YOU.
AS YOU SAY, M'LORD.
YOU ARE AWARE THAT THOSE VANQUISHED IN THE TOURNEY FORFEIT THEIR ARMS, ARMOR AND HORSE TO THE VICTORS, AND MUST RANSOM THEM BACK?
I KNOW.
AND YOU HAVE COIN TO PAY SUCH A RANSOM?
I WON'T HAVE **NEED** OF COIN.

BOLD WORDS, BUT TRUE. IF I WON MY FIRST TILT, I'D HAVE THE LOSER'S ARMOR AND HORSE -- OR HIS GOLD -- AND I COULD STAND A LOSS MYSELF.
WHO ARE THEY?
CAN'T YOU SEE THE BANNERS?
BUT TO BE ABLE TO TILT AT ALL, I DID HAVE NEED OF COIN.
HOUSE TARGARYEN.
THE LINE OF THE DRAGONKINGS.
STABLEBOY!
SER?
I MUST SPEAK WITH LORD ASHFORD'S MASTER OF HORSE.
I'LL FIND HIM FOR YOU.
AND WITH THEM, THE KINGSGUARD KNIGHTS --
-- WITH THE ROYAL BANNER.
BOY!
LET GO OF THAT NAG AND SEE TO MY HORSE!

BOY!
I SAID LET GO OF THAT NAG AND SEE TO MY HORSE!
ME?
I AM NOT A STABLEBOY, M'LORD.
NOT CLEVER ENOUGH, EH?
IF YOU CANNOT MANAGE A HORSE, FETCH ME SOME WINE AND A PRETTY WENCH!
M'LORD, I'M NOT A SERVING MAN EITHER.
I HAVE THE HONOR TO BE A KNIGHT.
KNIGHTHOOD HAS FALLEN ON SAD DAYS.
YOU!
BOY!
I NEED MY HORSE TAKEN CARE OF AND A WENCH TO TAKE CARE OF ME...
YOU ASKED TO SEE ME?

YES, M'LORD.
WHAT IS IT?
I WANT TO SELL THIS PALFREY.
SHE'S A GOOD HORSE, SURE OF FOOT --
I HAVE NO TIME FOR THIS AND MY LORD HAS NO NEED!
TAKE HER INTO TOWN, PERHAPS HENLY WILL GIVE YOU SOMETHING.
THANK YOU, M'LORD.
M'LORD, HAS THE KING COME?
HAHA!
NO, THANK THE GODS.
THIS INFESTATION OF PRINCES IS TRIAL ENOUGH!
WHERE AM I GOING TO FIND THE STALLS FOR ALL THESE ANIMALS!
AND FODDER!

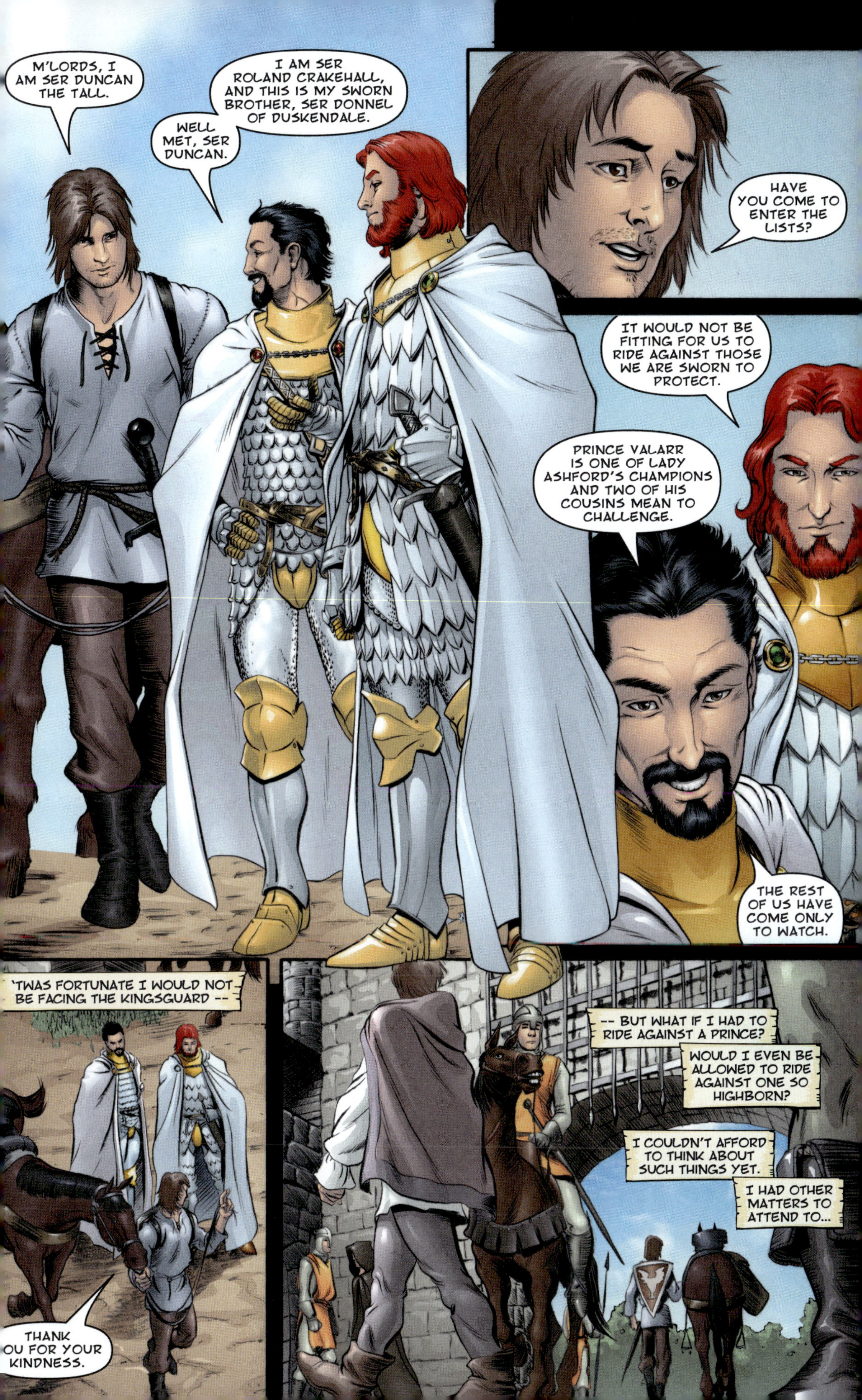
M'LORDS, I AM SER DUNCAN THE TALL.
I AM SER ROLAND CRAKEHALL, AND THIS IS MY SWORN BROTHER, SER DONNEL OF DUSKENDALE.
WELL MET, SER DUNCAN.
HAVE YOU COME TO ENTER THE LISTS?
IT WOULD NOT BE FITTING FOR US TO RIDE AGAINST THOSE WE ARE SWORN TO PROTECT.
PRINCE VALARR IS ONE OF LADY ASHFORD'S CHAMPIONS AND TWO OF HIS COUSINS MEAN TO CHALLENGE.
THE REST OF US HAVE COME ONLY TO WATCH.
'TWAS FORTUNATE I WOULD NOT BE FACING THE KINGSGUARD --
THANK OU FOR YOUR KINDNESS.
-- BUT WHAT IF I HAD TO RIDE AGAINST A PRINCE?
WOULD I EVEN BE ALLOWED TO RIDE AGAINST ONE SO HIGHBORN?
I COULDN'T AFFORD TO THINK ABOUT SUCH THINGS YET.
I HAD OTHER MATTERS TO ATTEND TO...

THE OLD MAN ALWAYS SAID THAT A KNIGHT SHOULD NEVER LOVE A HORSE, SINCE MORE THAN A FEW WERE LIKE TO DIE UNDER HIM.
WHAT CAN I DO FOR YE?
THIS IS SWEETFOOT.
AH, A FINE LOOKING BEAST! STRONG FLANKS. PROUD GAIT.
AND HOW MUCH WOULD YOU GIVE ME FOR HER?
WELL, OF COURSE, SHE'S NOT PERFECT.
BOWED LEGS AND BACK. SEEMS TO BE LOSING HAIR. HURRM. FLEAS.
HUHNH... THREE HUNDRED SILVERS.
THREE HUNDRED! MORE LIKE THREE THOUSAND!
SER, PLEASE, NOT EVEN IN HER PRIME... FIVE HUNDRED.
TWO THOUSAND.
ONE THOUSAND?
PERHAPS THERE ARE OTHER STABLEMEN ABOUT WHO ARE AS STUPID AS YOU SEEM TO THINK I AM -- GO TO THEM.
SEVEN HUNDRED AND FIFTY. FINAL OFFER.
VERY WELL.
SWEETFOOT HAD BORNE SER ARLAN TIRELESSLY OVER THOUSANDS OF MILES, ALL UP AND DOWN THE SEVEN KINGDOMS.
THE EXTRA'S FOR HER.
SEE THAT SHE HAS SOME OATS TONIGHT.
AND AN APPLE, TOO!
BUT THE OLD MAN NEVER HEEDED HIS OWN COUNSEL ABOUT HIS HORSES.
WHY SHOULD I?

SEVEN HUNDRED ND FIFTY SILVERS.
I COULD HAVE LIVED A YEAR ON THAT MONEY.
BUT WHAT THEN, WHEN IT WAS GONE?
..DOWN THE ROAD FROM HERE TO THERE!
FROM HERE! TO THERE!
THREE BOYS, A GOAT, AND A DANCING BEAR
HAVE AT YE!
SELL THE OTHER HORSES?
THAT ROAD ENDED IN BEGGARY OR OUTLAWRY -- THIS CHANCE WOULD NEVER COME AGAIN, I HAD TO RISK IT ALL.
AND THE KNIGHT RAISED HIS SWORD AS THE DRAGON LUNGED, TEETH BARED.
AND THEN --
RAAAHHRRR
AND WITH THAT SINGLE LUCKY STROKE, SER RILIAN SLEW THE BEAST AND WAS ABLE TO RETURN HOME AND TAKE HIS RIGHTFUL PLACE AS PRINCE!
AAAH!
HAHAHA!
HURRAH!
SAWDUST? HAHAHA!

GOOD SHOW!
HERE -- AND ONE FOR LAST NIGHT.
HER SMILE WAS AS SWEE AS ANY I'D EVER SEEN.
ALTHOUGH I WONDERED IF IT WAS ME SHE SMILED AT, OR THE COINS.
UH, WILL YOU DRINK A HORN OF ALE?
WITH ME, I MEAN?
OR A SAUSAGE?
I HAD A SAUSAGE LAST NIGHT, AND IT WAS GOOD.
THEY'RE MADE OF PORK, I THINK...
I THANK YOU, M'LORD, BUT WE HAVE ANOTHER SHOW.
YES, OF COURSE...
SHE WAS A PRETTY GIRL, AND TALL.
I WOULD NOT HAVE TO KNEEL T KISS THAT ONE...
...I CALLED FOR A KNIGHT, BUT YOU'RE A BEAR!
A BEAR! A BEAR! ALL BLACK AND BROWN AND COVERED IN HAIR...
I WAS BEING A FOOL.

IT WAS JOUSTING I SHOULD HAVE BEEN THINKING OF, NOT KISSING.
HEE-YEAAAH!
KICK HIS ARSE!
GET 'IM!
CRUNK
YEAH!
HUNH
UHN
CRAAACK

COME, NOW, COUSIN!
RAYMUN, DO SOMETHING!
HAHAHA!
NOT FAIR!
OOOF!
YIELD?
KRUNK
NO I DO NOT!

CRUNK
HERE'S AN APPLE THAT'S NOT RIPE YET!
I NEED SOMEONE NEW TO CROSS SWORDS WITH.
DO IT, SER DUNCAN!
I MAY NOT BE RIPE, BUT MY GOOD COUSIN IS ROTTEN TO THE CORE!
YOU THERE-- IS THAT A LONGSWORD YOU WEAR?
IT IS MINE BY RIGHTS.
I AM SER DUNCAN THE TALL.
AND I SER STEFFON FOSSOWAY.
I THANK YOU, SER, BUT I HAVE MATTERS TO ATTEND TO.
THE HEDGE KNIGHT HAS *MATTERS*.
WHY WERE THESE LORDLINGS INCLUDING ME IN THEIR QUARREL?
SER GRANCE, COME TRY ME!
I KNOW EVERY FEEBLE TRICK MY COUSIN HAS MASTERED, AND SER DUNCAN NEEDS TO RETURN TO THE HEDGES!
I DID NOT HAVE MANY TRICKS MYSELF, FEEBLE OR OTHERWISE, AND I DID NOT WANT ANYONE TO SEE ME FIGHT UNTIL THE TOURNEY.

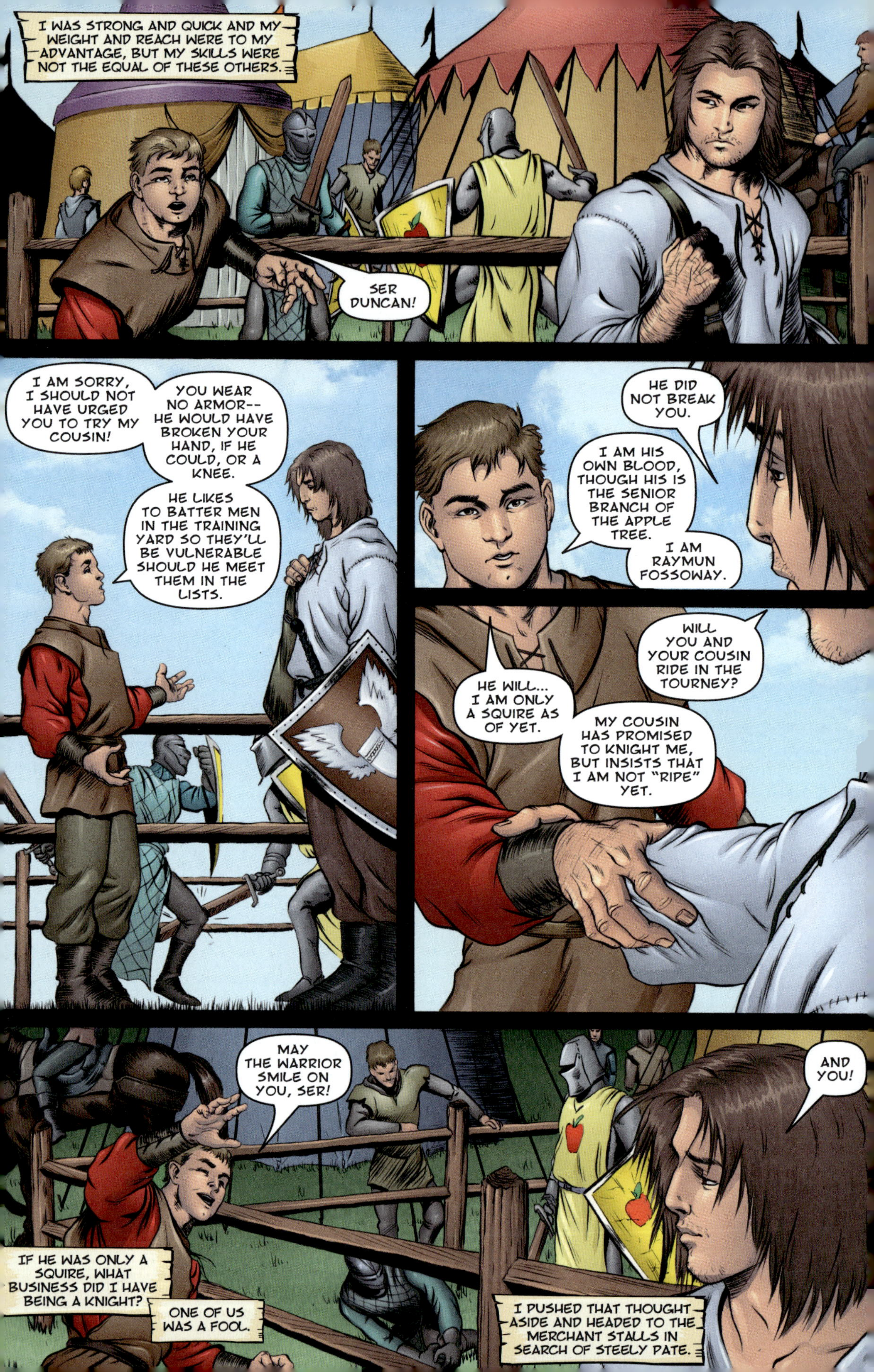
I WAS STRONG AND QUICK AND MY WEIGHT AND REACH WERE TO MY ADVANTAGE, BUT MY SKILLS WERE NOT THE EQUAL OF THESE OTHERS.
SER DUNCAN!
I AM SORRY, I SHOULD NOT HAVE URGED YOU TO TRY MY COUSIN!
YOU WEAR NO ARMOR-- HE WOULD HAVE BROKEN YOUR HAND, IF HE COULD, OR A KNEE.
HE LIKES TO BATTER MEN IN THE TRAINING YARD SO THEY'LL BE VULNERABLE SHOULD HE MEET THEM IN THE LISTS.
HE DID NOT BREAK YOU.
I AM HIS OWN BLOOD, THOUGH HIS IS THE SENIOR BRANCH OF THE APPLE TREE.
I AM RAYMUN FOSSOWAY.
WILL YOU AND YOUR COUSIN RIDE IN THE TOURNEY?
HE WILL... I AM ONLY A SQUIRE AS OF YET.
MY COUSIN HAS PROMISED TO KNIGHT ME, BUT INSISTS THAT I AM NOT "RIPE" YET.
MAY THE WARRIOR SMILE ON YOU, SER!
AND YOU!
IF HE WAS ONLY A SQUIRE, WHAT BUSINESS DID I HAVE BEING A KNIGHT?
ONE OF US WAS A FOOL.
I PUSHED THAT THOUGHT ASIDE AND HEADED TO THE MERCHANT STALLS IN SEARCH OF STEELY PATE.

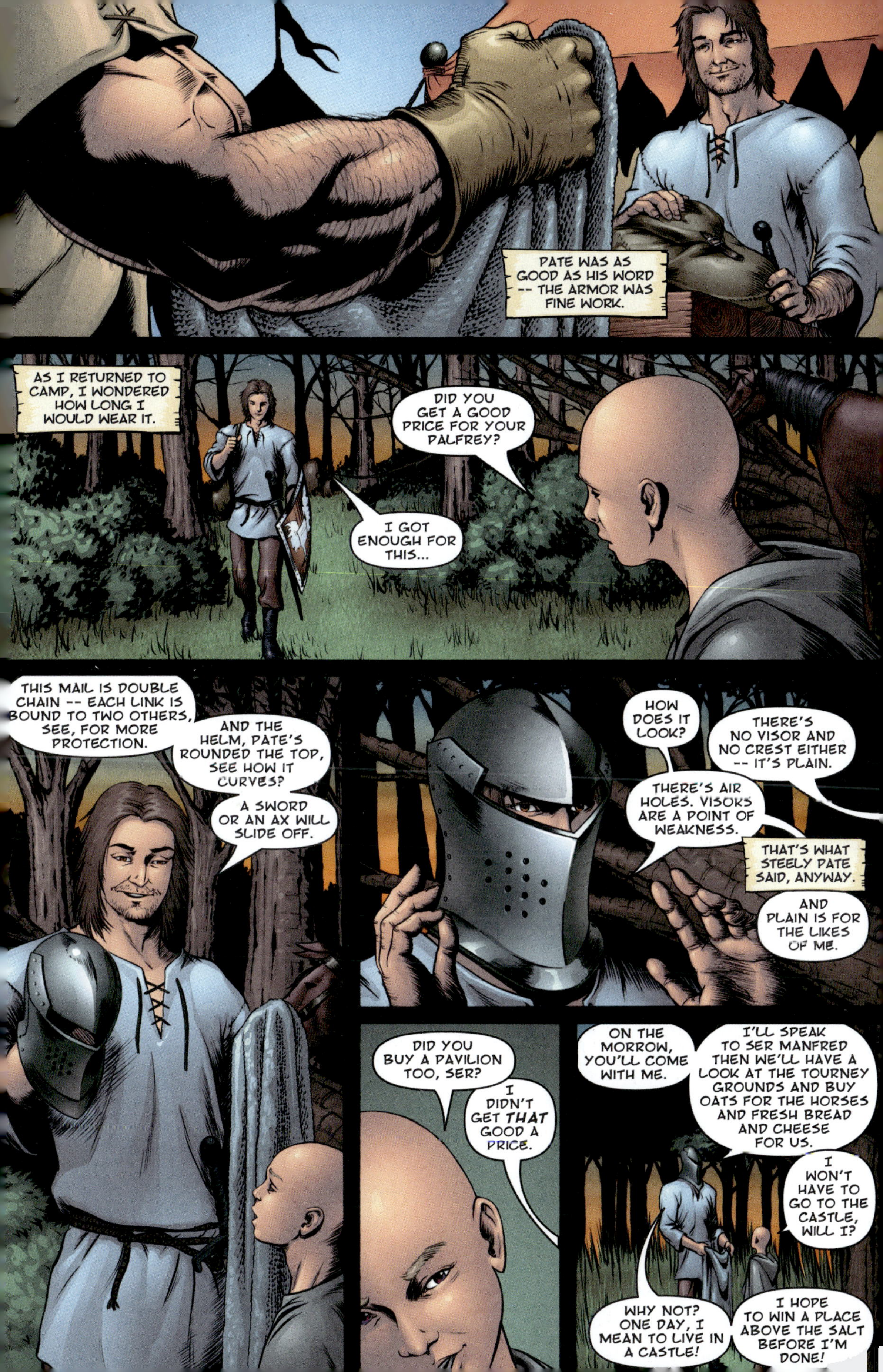
PATE WAS AS GOOD AS HIS WORD -- THE ARMOR WAS FINE WORK.
AS I RETURNED TO CAMP, I WONDERED HOW LONG I WOULD WEAR IT.
DID YOU GET A GOOD PRICE FOR YOUR PALFREY?
I GOT ENOUGH FOR THIS...
THIS MAIL IS DOUBLE CHAIN -- EACH LINK IS BOUND TO TWO OTHERS, SEE, FOR MORE PROTECTION.
AND THE HELM, PATE'S ROUNDED THE TOP, SEE HOW IT CURVES?
A SWORD OR AN AX WILL SLIDE OFF.
HOW DOES IT LOOK?
THERE'S NO VISOR AND NO CREST EITHER -- IT'S PLAIN.
THERE'S AIR HOLES. VISORS ARE A POINT OF WEAKNESS.
THAT'S WHAT STEELY PATE SAID, ANYWAY.
AND PLAIN IS FOR THE LIKES OF ME.
DID YOU BUY A PAVILION TOO, SER?
I DIDN'T GET THAT GOOD A PRICE.
ON THE MORROW, YOU'LL COME WITH ME.
I'LL SPEAK TO SER MANFRED THEN WE'LL HAVE A LOOK AT THE TOURNEY GROUNDS AND BUY OATS FOR THE HORSES AND FRESH BREAD AND CHEESE FOR US.
I WON'T HAVE TO GO TO THE CASTLE, WILL I?
WHY NOT? ONE DAY, I MEAN TO LIVE IN A CASTLE!
I HOPE TO WIN A PLACE ABOVE THE SALT BEFORE I'M DONE!

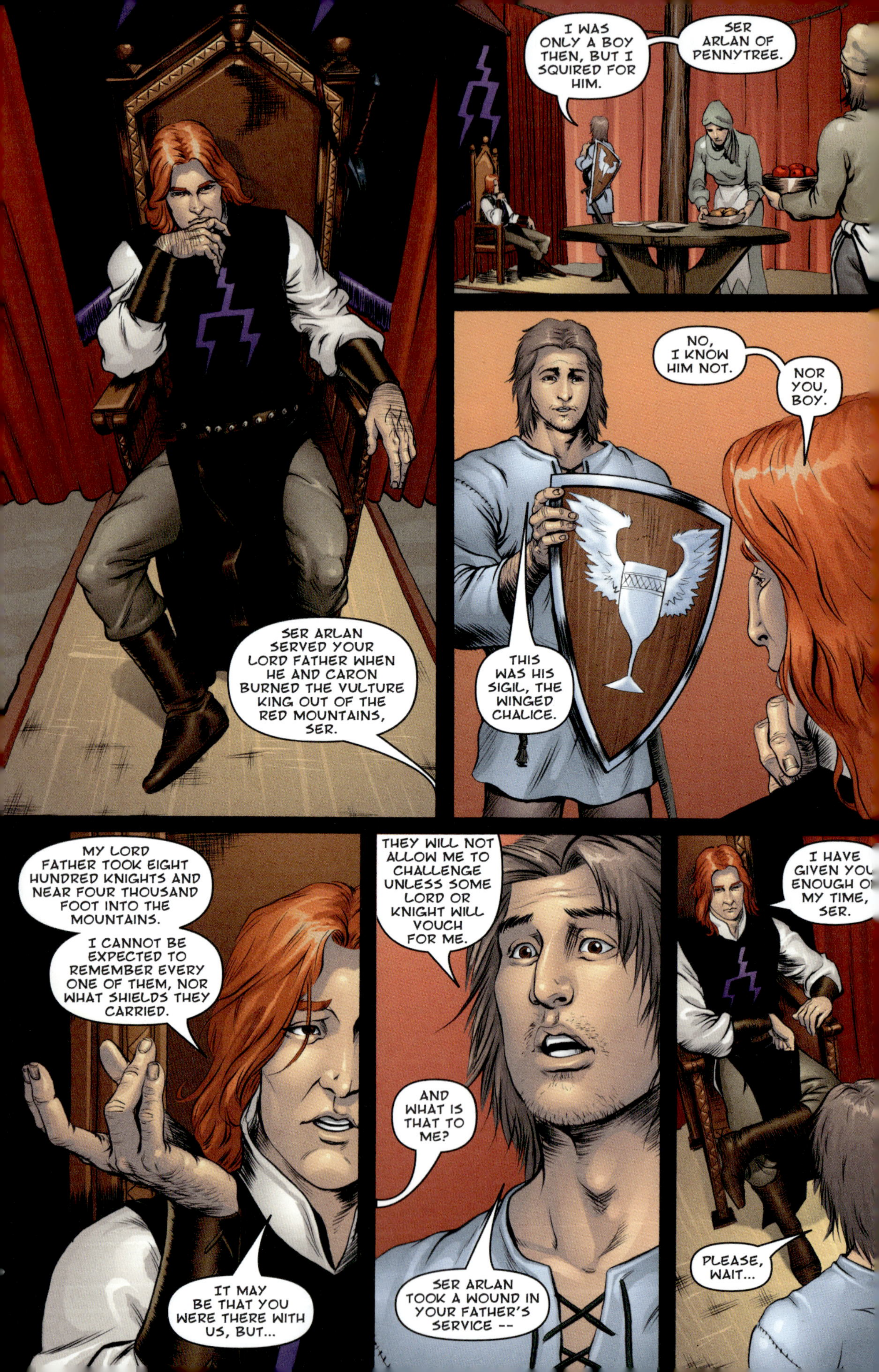
I WAS ONLY A BOY THEN, BUT I SQUIRED FOR HIM.
SER ARLAN OF PENNYTREE.
SER ARLAN SERVED YOUR LORD FATHER WHEN HE AND CARON BURNED THE VULTURE KING OUT OF THE RED MOUNTAINS, SER.
NO, I KNOW HIM NOT.
NOR YOU, BOY.
THIS WAS HIS SIGIL, THE WINGED CHALICE.
MY LORD FATHER TOOK EIGHT HUNDRED KNIGHTS AND NEAR FOUR THOUSAND FOOT INTO THE MOUNTAINS.
I CANNOT BE EXPECTED TO REMEMBER EVERY ONE OF THEM, NOR WHAT SHIELDS THEY CARRIED.
IT MAY BE THAT YOU WERE THERE WITH US, BUT...
THEY WILL NOT ALLOW ME TO CHALLENGE UNLESS SOME LORD OR KNIGHT WILL VOUCH FOR ME.
AND WHAT IS THAT TO ME?
SER ARLAN TOOK A WOUND IN YOUR FATHER'S SERVICE --
I HAVE GIVEN YOU ENOUGH OF MY TIME, SER.
PLEASE, WAIT...

"HE SAID THAT ONE STORMY NIGHT, AN ARROW KILLED THE HORSE OF A MESSENGER.
"TWO DORNISHMEN CAME OUT OF THE DARKNESS IN RING MAIL AND CRESTED HELMS.
"HIS SWORD BROKEN IN THE FALL, THE MESSENGER THOUGHT HE WAS DOOMED.
I REMEMBER OUR FATHER ELLING THE CAMP HOW OUR HOUSE GOT ITS SIGIL.
"BUT AS THEY CLOSED IN, LIGHTNING -- BRIGHT PURPLE BURNING LIGHTNING -- CRACKED FROM THE SKY, STRIKING THE DORNISHMEN IN THEIR STEEL AND KILLING THEM WHERE THEY STOOD!
"THE MESSAGE GAVE THE STORM KING VICTORY OVER THE DORNISH AND IN THANKS HE RAISED THE MESSENGER UP TO LORDSHIP."
SO HE TOOK FOR HIS ARMS THE PURPLE LIGHTNING.
WHAT WAS YOUR NAME AGAIN, SER?.
SER DUNK... DUNCAN THE TALL.
SER DUNCAN...

...EVERY POT BOY AND GROOM WHO HAS EVER SERVED MY FATHER HEARS THAT STORY SOONER OR LATER.
KNOWING IT DOES NOT MAKE YOU A KNIGHT.
BEGONE WITH YOU, SER!

ISSUE THREE
COVER A

MIKE S. MILLER

ISSUE THREE
COVER B

BORIS VALLEJO AND JULIE BELL

IT WAS WITH A LEADEN HEART THAT I RETURNED TO ASHFORD CASTLE, WONDERING WHAT I MIGHT SAY SO THAT PLUMMER WOULD GRANT ME THE RIGHT OF CHALLENGE.
PLUMMER!
KNOCK KNOCK
MASTER PLUMMER?
WHERE CAN I FIND PLUMMER?
I BELIEVE HE CAN BE FOUND IN THE GREAT HALL.
SHALL I WAIT HERE?
HOW SHOULD I KNOW?
DO WHAT YOU PLEASE.

THE GREAT HALL WAS NOT SO GREAT, AS HALLS WENT, BUT ASHFORD WAS A SMALL CASTLE.
YOU WOULD BE MORE CONCERNED IF THEY WERE YOUR SONS, I'LL WAGER.
DAERON HAS DONE THIS BEFORE.
YOU SHOULD NEVER HAVE COMMANDED HIM TO ENTER THE LISTS.
HE BELONGS ON A TOURNEY FIELD NO MORE THAN AERYS DOES, OR RHAEGEL.
BY WHICH YOU MEAN HE'D SOONER RIDE A WHORE THAN A HORSE!
I DO NOT NEED TO BE REMINDED OF MY SON'S FAILINGS, BROTHER.
DAERON IS WHAT HE IS, BUT HE IS STILL YOUR BLOOD AND MINE.
I HAVE NO DOUBT SER ROLAND WILL TURN HIM UP, AND AEGON WITH HIM.
WHEN THE TOURNEY IS OVER, PERHAPS...
IT CAME TO ME THAT I HAD WALKED IN ON SOMETHING I OUGHT NOT TO HAVE HEARD.
WHO ARE YOU AND WHAT DO YOU MEAN BY BURSTING IN ON US?
AH, HE IS THE KNIGHT OUR GOOD STEWARD WAS EXPECTING.
YOU AND I ARE THE INTRUDERS HERE, BROTHER.
COME CLOSER, SER.

MY LORDS...I... I ASKED SER MANFRED TO VOUCH FOR ME SO I MIGHT ENTER THE LISTS, BUT HE REFUSES -- HE SAYS HE KNOWS ME NOT.
SER ARLAN SERVED HIM, THOUGH, I SWEAR IT... I HAVE HIS SWORD AND SHIELD, I --
A SHIELD AND A SWORD DO NOT MAKE A KNIGHT.
PLUMMER TOLD ME OF YOU. EVEN IF THESE ARMS BELONGED TO THIS SER ARLAN OF PENNYTREE, IT MAY WELL BE THAT YOU STOLE THEM.
I REMEMBER SER ARLAN OF PENNYTREE.
HE NEVER WON A TOURNEY THAT I KNEW OF. BUT HE NEVER SHAMED HIMSELF EITHER.
SIXTEEN YEARS AGO, HE OVERTHREW LORD STOKEWORTH AND THE BASTARD OF HARRENHAL --
-- AND MANY YEARS BEFORE HE UNHORSED THE GREY LION HIMSELF!
HE TOLD ME ABOUT THAT, MANY A TIME!
THEN YOU WILL REMEMBER THE GREY KNIGHT'S TRUE NAME, I HAVE NO DOUBT.

SER DAMON LANNISTER.
THE GREY LION!
SER DAMON LANNISTER -- HE'S LORD OF CASTERLY ROCK NOW!
SO HE IS.
HOW CAN YOU POSSIBLY REMEMBER SOME INSIGNIFICANT **HEDGE KNIGHT** WHO CHANCED TO UNHORSE DAMON LANNISTER SIXTEEN YEARS AGO?
IT WAS NINE YEARS PAST, AT STORM'S END. THE LOTS MADE SER ARLAN MY OPPONENT IN THE FIRST TILT.
WE BROKE FOUR LANCES BEFORE IT WAS DONE.
SEVEN!
AND THAT WAS AGAINST THE PRINCE OF DRAGONSTONE!
I COULD ALMOST HEAR THE OLD MAN CHIDING, "DUNK THE LUNK, THICK AS A CASTLE WALL."

SO IT WAS. TALES GROW IN THE TELLING, I NOW. DO NOT THINK ILL OF YOUR OLD ASTER, BUT IT WAS FOUR LANCES ONLY.
MY LORD... ER... YOUR GRACE...
I NEVER... THE OLD MAN, SER ARLAN, HE USED TO SAY I WAS SLOW AS AN AUROCHS.
AND STRONG S AN AUROCHS, BY THE LOOK OF YOU.
NO HARM WAS DONE, SER. RISE.
I WAS SPEAKING WITH BAELOR TARGARYEN, PRINCE OF DRAGONSTONE, HAND OF THE KING, AND HEIR APPARENT TO THE IRON THRONE OF AEGON THE CONQUEROR.
YOU WISH TO ENTER THE LISTS, IS THAT IT?
THAT DECISION RESTS WITH THE MASTER OF GAMES, BUT I SEE NO REASON TO DENY YOU.
AS YOU SAY, MY LORD.
THA--
VERY WELL, SER, YOU ARE GRATEFUL -- NOW BE OFF WITH YOU!
FORGIVE MY BROTHER, SER, TWO OF HIS SONS HAVE GONE ASTRAY ON THEIR WAY HERE AND HE FEARS FOR THEM.
I DID NOT COME HERE TO TAKE COUNSEL FROM A HEDGE KNIGHT.
THE SPRING RAINS HAVE SWOLLEN MANY STREAMS. PERHAPS THE PRINCES ARE ONLY DELAYED.
YOU MAY GO, SER.
SER, YOU ARE NOT OF SER ARLAN'S BLOOD?
NO, I'M NOT.
BY LAW, ONLY A TRUEBORN SON IS ENTITLED TO INHERIT A KNIGHT'S ARMS -- YOU MUST NEEDS FIND A SIGIL OF YOUR OWN.
THANK YOU AGAIN, YOUR GRACE.
I WILL FIGHT BRAVELY, YOU'LL SEE.

YOU ARE NO KNIGHT.
I KNOW YOU.
YOU ARE FLORIAN THE FOOL.
I AM, MY LADY.
AS GREAT A FOOL AS EVER LIVED, AND AS GREAT A KNIGHT AS WELL!
A FOOL AND A KNIGHT?
I HAVE NEVER HEARD OF SUCH A THING.
SWEET LADY, ALL MEN ARE FOOLS, AND ALL MEN ARE KNIGHTS, WHERE WOMEN ARE CONCERNED.
COME.

M'LORD?
THAT WAS GOOD! I LIKE HOW YOU MAKE THEM MOVE, JONQUIL AND THE DRAGON AND ALL.
I SAW A PUPPET SHOW LAST YEAR, BUT THEY MOVED ALL JERKY -- YOURS ARE MORE SMOOTH.
THANK YOU.
YOUR FIGURES ARE WELL CARVED TOO.
THE DRAGON, ESPECIALLY. YOU MAKE THEM YOURSELF?
MY UNCLE DOES THE CARVING; I PAINT THEM.
COULD YOU PAINT SOMETHING FOR ME?
I HAVE THE COIN TO PAY...
I NEED TO PAINT SOMETHING OVER THE CHALICE.
WHAT WOULD YOU WANT PAINTED?
I DON'T... I'M NOT CERTAIN.
"DUNK THE LUNK, THICK AS A CASTLE WALL."
YOU MUST THINK ME AN UTTER FOOL.
ALL MEN ARE FOOLS, AND ALL MEN ARE KNIGHTS.

WHAT COLOR PAINT DO YOU HAVE?
I CAN MIX ANY COLOR YOU WANT.
THE FIELD SHOULD BE THE COLOR OF SUNSET.
THE OLD MAN LIKED SUNSETS... AND THE DEVICE...
AN ELM TREE!
A BIG ELM TREE, LIKE THE ONE BY THE POOL, WITH A BROWN TRUNK AND GREEN BRANCHES!
YES... THAT WOULD SERVE. AN ELM TREE... BUT WITH A SHOOTING STAR ABOVE.
COULD YOU DO THAT?
GIVE ME THE SHIELD.
I'LL PAINT IT THIS VERY NIGHT, AND HAVE IT BACK TO YOU ON THE MORROW.
I AM CALLED SER DUNCAN THE TALL.
I'M TANSELLE.
TANSELLE TOO-TALL, THE BOYS USED TO CALL ME.
YOU'RE NOT TOO TALL, YOU'RE JUST RIGHT FOR...
FOR?
UH -- PUPPETS...

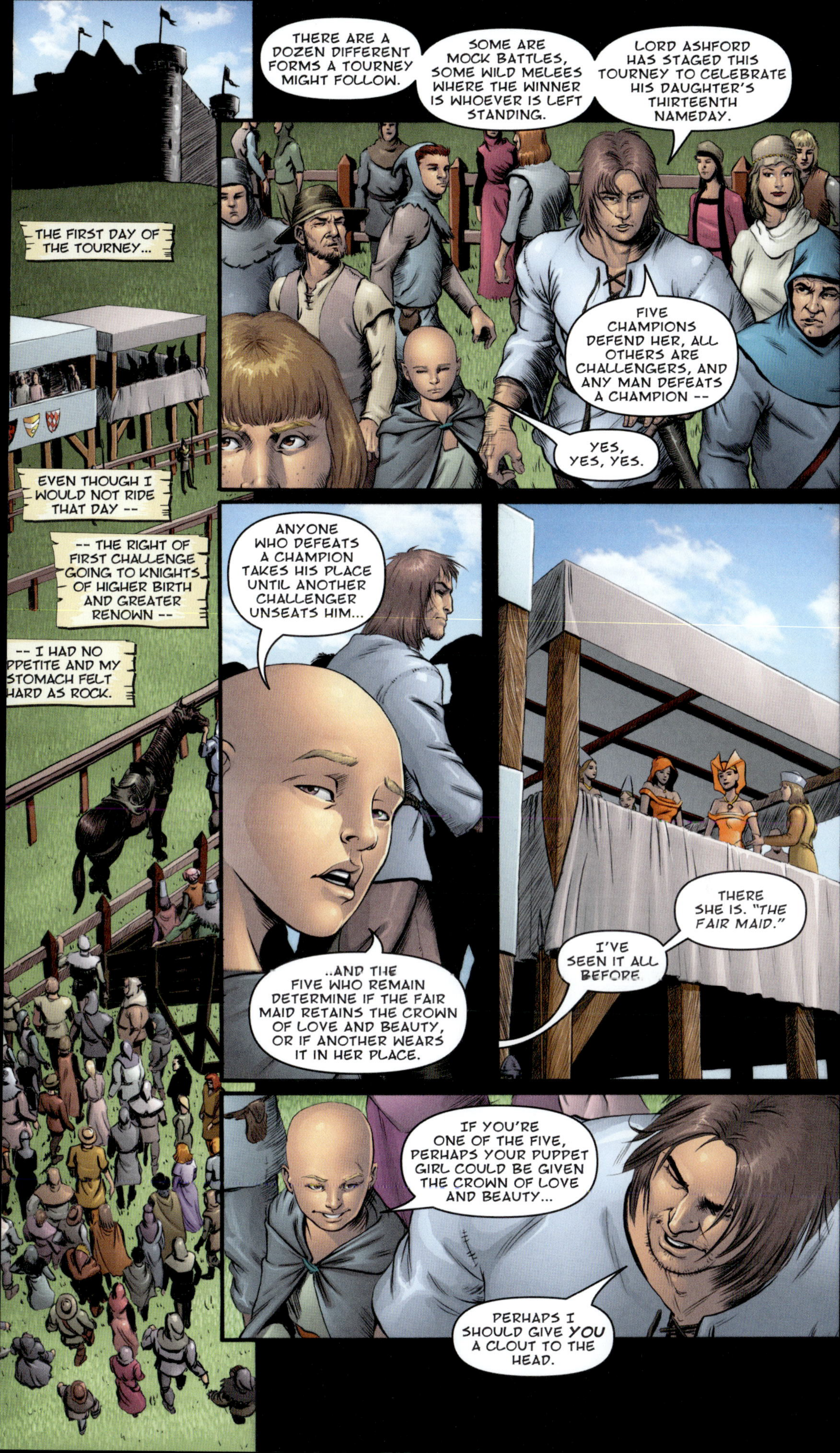
THE FIRST DAY OF THE TOURNEY...
THERE ARE A DOZEN DIFFERENT FORMS A TOURNEY MIGHT FOLLOW.
SOME ARE MOCK BATTLES, SOME WILD MELEES WHERE THE WINNER IS WHOEVER IS LEFT STANDING.
LORD ASHFORD HAS STAGED THIS TOURNEY TO CELEBRATE HIS DAUGHTER'S THIRTEENTH NAMEDAY.
FIVE CHAMPIONS DEFEND HER, ALL OTHERS ARE CHALLENGERS, AND ANY MAN DEFEATS A CHAMPION --
YES, YES, YES.
EVEN THOUGH I WOULD NOT RIDE THAT DAY --
-- THE RIGHT OF FIRST CHALLENGE GOING TO KNIGHTS OF HIGHER BIRTH AND GREATER RENOWN --
-- I HAD NO PPETITE AND MY STOMACH FELT HARD AS ROCK.
ANYONE WHO DEFEATS A CHAMPION TAKES HIS PLACE UNTIL ANOTHER CHALLENGER UNSEATS HIM...
..AND THE FIVE WHO REMAIN DETERMINE IF THE FAIR MAID RETAINS THE CROWN OF LOVE AND BEAUTY, OR IF ANOTHER WEARS IT IN HER PLACE.
THERE SHE IS. "THE FAIR MAID."
I'VE SEEN IT ALL BEFORE
IF YOU'RE ONE OF THE FIVE, PERHAPS YOUR PUPPET GIRL COULD BE GIVEN THE CROWN OF LOVE AND BEAUTY...
PERHAPS I SHOULD GIVE YOU A CLOUT TO THE HEAD.

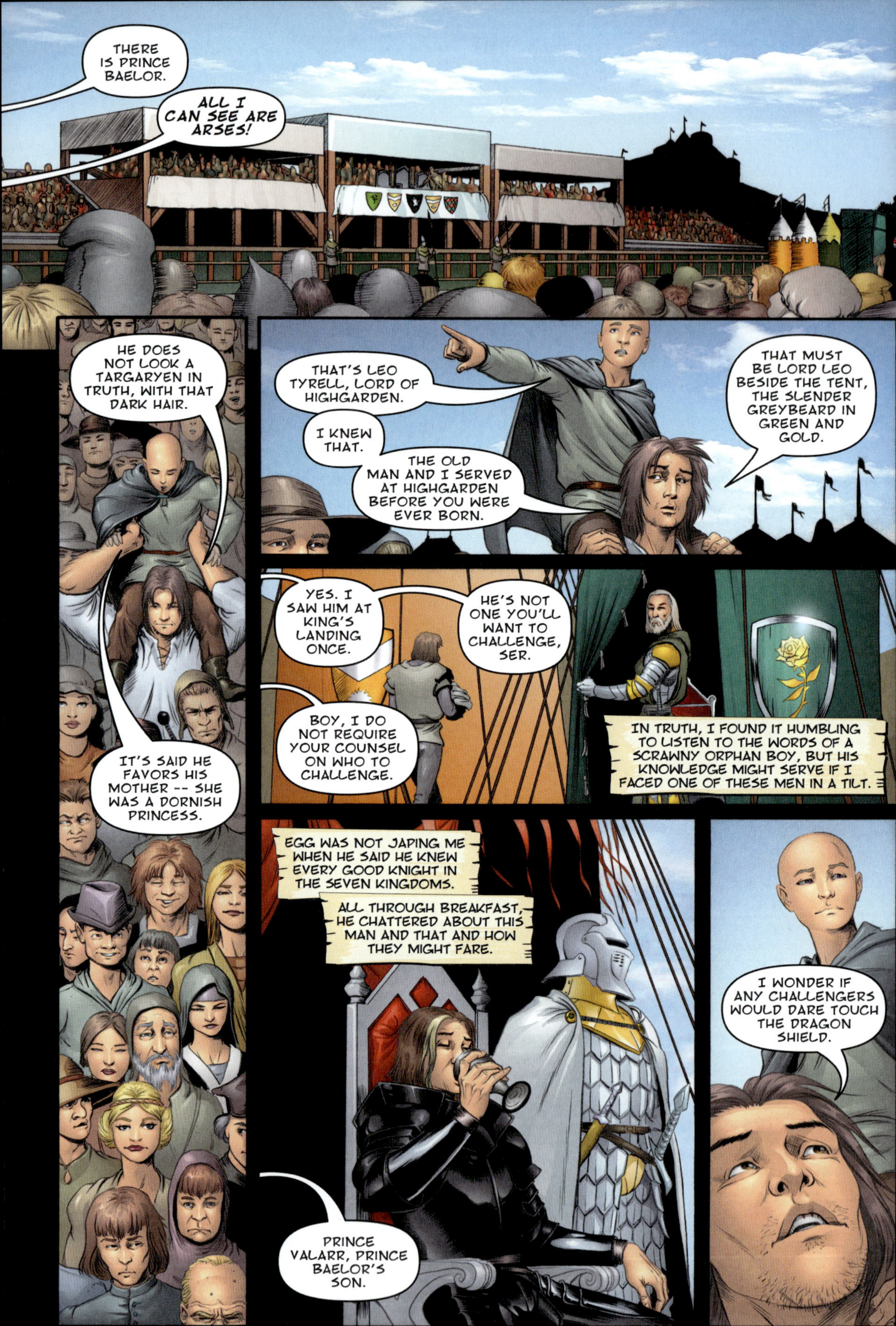
THERE IS PRINCE BAELOR.
ALL I CAN SEE ARE ARSES!
HE DOES NOT LOOK A TARGARYEN IN TRUTH, WITH THAT DARK HAIR.
IT'S SAID HE FAVORS HIS MOTHER -- SHE WAS A DORNISH PRINCESS.
THAT'S LEO TYRELL, LORD OF HIGHGARDEN.
I KNEW THAT.
THE OLD MAN AND I SERVED AT HIGHGARDEN BEFORE YOU WERE EVER BORN.
THAT MUST BE LORD LEO BESIDE THE TENT, THE SLENDER GREYBEARD IN GREEN AND GOLD.
YES. I SAW HIM AT KING'S LANDING ONCE.
HE'S NOT ONE YOU'LL WANT TO CHALLENGE, SER.
BOY, I DO NOT REQUIRE YOUR COUNSEL ON WHO TO CHALLENGE.
IN TRUTH, I FOUND IT HUMBLING TO LISTEN TO THE WORDS OF A SCRAWNY ORPHAN BOY, BUT HIS KNOWLEDGE MIGHT SERVE IF I FACED ONE OF THESE MEN IN A TILT.
EGG WAS NOT JAPING ME WHEN HE SAID HE KNEW EVERY GOOD KNIGHT IN THE SEVEN KINGDOMS.
ALL THROUGH BREAKFAST, HE CHATTERED ABOUT THIS MAN AND THAT AND HOW THEY MIGHT FARE.
PRINCE VALARR, PRINCE BAELOR'S SON.
I WONDER IF ANY CHALLENGERS WOULD DARE TOUCH THE DRAGON SHIELD.

THE HORNS BLEW AND HERALDS BOOMED OUT THE NAME OF EACH CHALLENGER IN TURN.
THEY PAUSED BEFORE THE VIEWING STAND TO DIP THEIR LANCES IN SALUTE TO LORD ASHFORD, PRINCE BAELOR, AND THE FAIR MAID.
THEN SELECTED THEIR OPPONENT BY TAPPING ONE OF THE CHAMPION'S SHIELDS WITH THEIR LANCE.
AS THE KNIGHTS TROTTED INTO POSITION, ASHFORD MEADOW GREW ALMOST STILL.

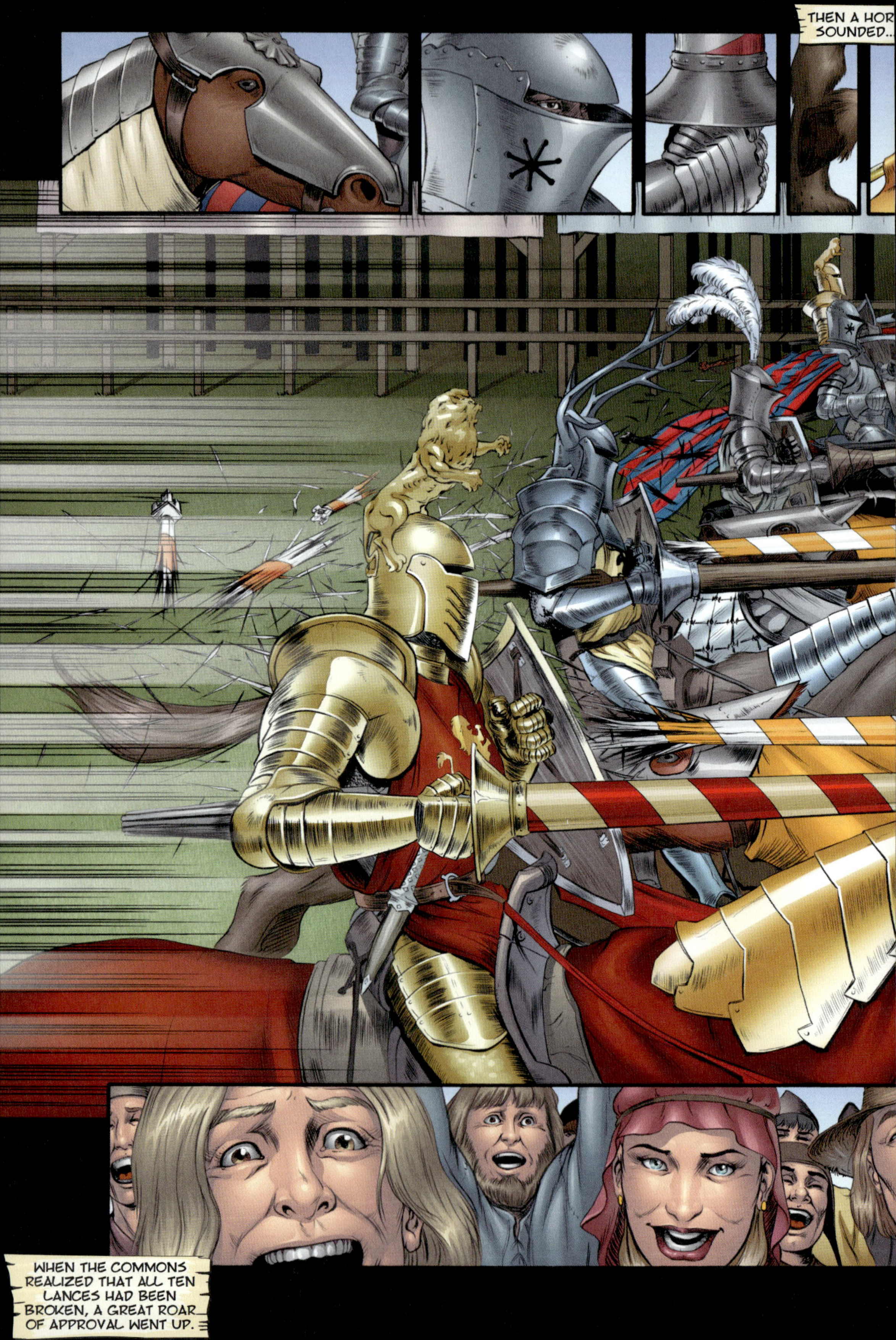
THEN A HOR
SOUNDED...
WHEN THE COMMONS REALIZED THAT ALL TEN LANCES HAD BEEN BROKEN, A GREAT ROAR OF APPROVAL WENT UP.

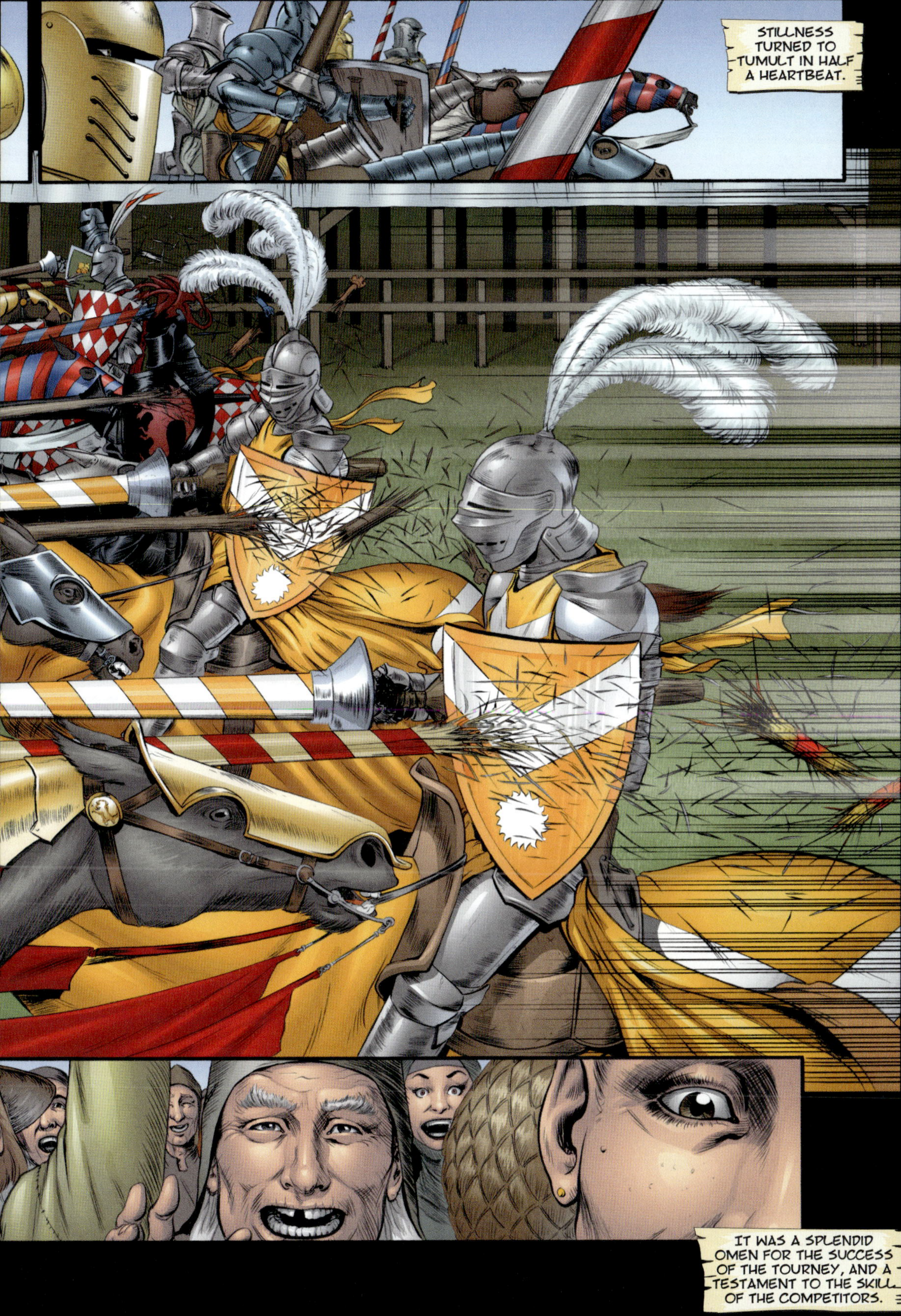
STILLNESS TURNED TO TUMULT IN HALF A HEARTBEAT.
IT WAS A SPLENDID OMEN FOR THE SUCCESS OF THE TOURNEY, AND A TESTAMENT TO THE SKILL OF THE COMPETITORS.

IT WAS, SMALL FOLK AND HIGH FOLK AGREED, A SPLENDID DAY OF JOUSTING.
SER HUMFREY HARDYN AND SER HUMFREY BEESBURY SPLINTERE NO LESS THAN A DOZE LANCES APIECE.
THE SMALLFOLK SOON BEGAN CALLING THE EPIC STRUGGLE "THE BATTLE OF HUMFREY".
ONE EYED SER ROBYN RHYSLIN LOST HIS HELM T LORD LEO'S LANC IN THEIR FIRST COURSE, BUT H REFUSED TO YIEL
THREE TIMES MORE THEY RODE AT EACH OTHER.
ALL THE MORE IMPRESSIVE SINC SER ROBYN HAD LOST HIS EYE TO A SPLINTER FRO A BROKEN LANC NOT FIVE YEARS EARLIER.
LEO TYRELL WAS TO CHIVALROUS TO AI ANOTHER LANCE AT SER ROBYN'S HEAD BUT SER ROBYN'S STUBBORN COURAG (OR WAS IT FOLLY? LEFT ME ASTOUNDE

I FOUND MYSELF WONDERING IF PRINCE VALARR HAD INHERITED A MEASURE OF HIS FATHER'S PROWESS AFTER HE DEFEATED HIS FIRST FEW CHALLENGERS.
EGG, WHO IS THE LEAST DANGEROUS OF THESE CHALLENGERS?
LORD GAWEN. VALARR'S FOE.
PRINCE VALARR.
A SQUIRE MUST KEEP A COURTEOUS TONGUE, BOY.
WELL FOUGHT
WELL FOUGHT.
I YIELD, YOUR GRACE.
WELL FOUGHT.
IT WAS NOT EITHER!
BE QUIET, OR YOU CAN GO BACK TO CAMP.

HAHAHA
SER LYONEL BARATHEON ALSO FOUGHT SEVERAL NOTABLE MATCHES.
HAHAHAHA
AGAINST LESSER FOES, HE WOULD OFTEN BREAK INTO BOOMING LAUGHTE THE MOMENT THEY TOUCHED HIS SHIEL
HAHAHA
AND LAUGH ALL THE TIME HE WAS CHARGING AND KNOCKING THEM FROM THEIR STIRRUPS.
HAHAHA HAHAHAHA

IF HIS CHALLENGERS WORE ANY SORT OF CREST ON THEIR HELM --
HAHAHA
-- SER LYONEL WOULD STRIKE IT OFF AND FLING IT INTO THE CROWD.
KRAANG
THE MEN HE BEAT DID NOT APPRECIATE THE HABIT.
IT MADE HIM A GREAT FAVORITE OF THE COMMONS, THOUGH.
I YIELD!
HEH...
BEFORE LONG, ONLY CRESTLESS MEN WERE CHALLENGING HIM, THOUGH.
AS OFTEN AS SER LYONEL LAUGHED DOWN A CHALLENGER, I THOUGHT THE DAYS HONORS BELONGED TO SER HUMFREY HARDYNG, WHO HUMBLED FOURTEEN KNIGHTS, EACH FORMIDABLE.
MEANWHILE, THE YOUNG PRINCE SAT OUTSIDE HIS BLACK PAVILION, RISING FROM TIME TO TIME TO MOUNT HIS HORSE AND VANQUISH YET ANOTHER UNDISTINGUISHED FOE.
HE HAD NINE VICTORIES -- OLD MEN AND UPJUMPED SQUIRES -- BUT THE TRULY DANGEROUS FOES RODE PAST HIS SHIELD AS IF THEY DIDN'T SEE IT.

LATE IN THE DAY, A BRAZEN FANFARE ANNOUNCED A NEW CHALLENGER TO THE LISTS.
PRINCE AERION BRIGHTFLAME OF THE RED KEEP OF KING'S LANDING --
-- SON OF MAEKAR PRINCE OF SUMMERHALL OF HOUSE TARGARYEN --
-- GRANDSON TO DAERON THE GOOD --
-- THE SECOND OF HIS NAME --
-- KING OF THE ANDALS, THE RYONAR, AND THE FIRST MEN --
-- AND LORD OF THE SEVEN KINGDOMS!
FOR A MOMENT, I WAS SURE THAT AERION MEANT TO STRIKE VALARR'S SHIELD . . .
VALARR THOUGHT SO AS WELL.
INSTEAD, HE CHOSE SER HUMFREY.
COME OUT, COME OUT, LITTLE KNIGHT!
IT'S TIME YOU FACED THE DRAGON!

SER HUMFREY BROKE SLOWLY, BUILDING SPEED --
-- BUT AERION RAKED HIS CHARGER WITH BOTH SPURS, COMING HARD.
KILL HIM!
HE'S RIGHT THERE!
KILL HIM!
KILL HIM!
KILL HIM!
I WAS NOT SURE WHICH OF THE KNIGHTS EGG WAS SHOUTING TO.
STOP! DO YOU MEAN TO CHOKE ME!
LOW, TOO LOW.
HE'LL MISS THE RIDER AND STRIKE SER HUMFREY'S HORSE.
HE CAN'T MEAN TO...

SPLEERCH

THE CHEERS OF ASHFORD MEADOW WERE REPLACED WITH SHOUTING AND SCREAMING.
ABOVE IT ALL, THOUGH, WERE THE SCREAMS OF THE DYING HORSE.
WEEEERGH

LET ME DOWN.
THAT POOR HORSE...
LET ME DOWN!
THE HORSE'S SCREAMS WERE ALMOST HUMAN.
WEEERGH
I WONDERED WHAT I WOULD DO IF SUCH A FATE BEFELL THUNDER.
POOR, POOR HORSE..
A TERRIBLE SIGHT, AYE, BUT A SQUIRE MUST NEEDS BE STRONG.
YOU'LL SEE WORSE MISHAPS AT OTHER TOURNEYS, I FEAR.
IT WAS NO MISHAP.
AERION MEANT TO DO IT.
YOU SAW.
IT HAD LOOKED THAT WAY TO ME AS WELL.
BUT I COULD NOT ACCEPT THAT ANY KNIGHT COULD BE SO UNCHIVALROUS, LEAST OF ALL ONE WHO WAS BLOOD OF THE DRAGON.
I SAW A KNIGHT GREEN AS SUMMER GRASS LOSE CONTROL OF HIS LANCE, AND I'LL HEAR NO MORE OF IT.
THE JOUSTING IS DONE FOR THE DAY, I THINK. COME, LAD.

ISSUE FOUR
COVER A

MIKE S. MILLER

ISSUE FOUR
COVER B

TOM YEATES

THANK YOU.
I HAD BEEN RIGHT ABOUT THE END OF THE DAY'S CONTESTS.
BY THE TIME THE CHAOS HAD BEEN SET TO RIGHTS, THE SUN WAS LOW IN THE WEST, AND LORD ASHFORD HAD CALLED A HALT.
I BOUGHT EGG HALF A HORN OF ALE, HOPING TO CHEER HIM.
COME.
PRINCE AERION'S ACCIDENTAL SLAYING OF THE HORSE -- EGG STILL BELIEVED IT TO BE INTENTIONAL -- WEIGHED HEAVILY ON THE BOY.
WE WANDERED FOR A TIME...
...LISTENED TO A SPRIGHTLY AIR ON PIPES AND DRUM...
...AND THEN --
I KNOW WHAT WILL CHEER YOU.

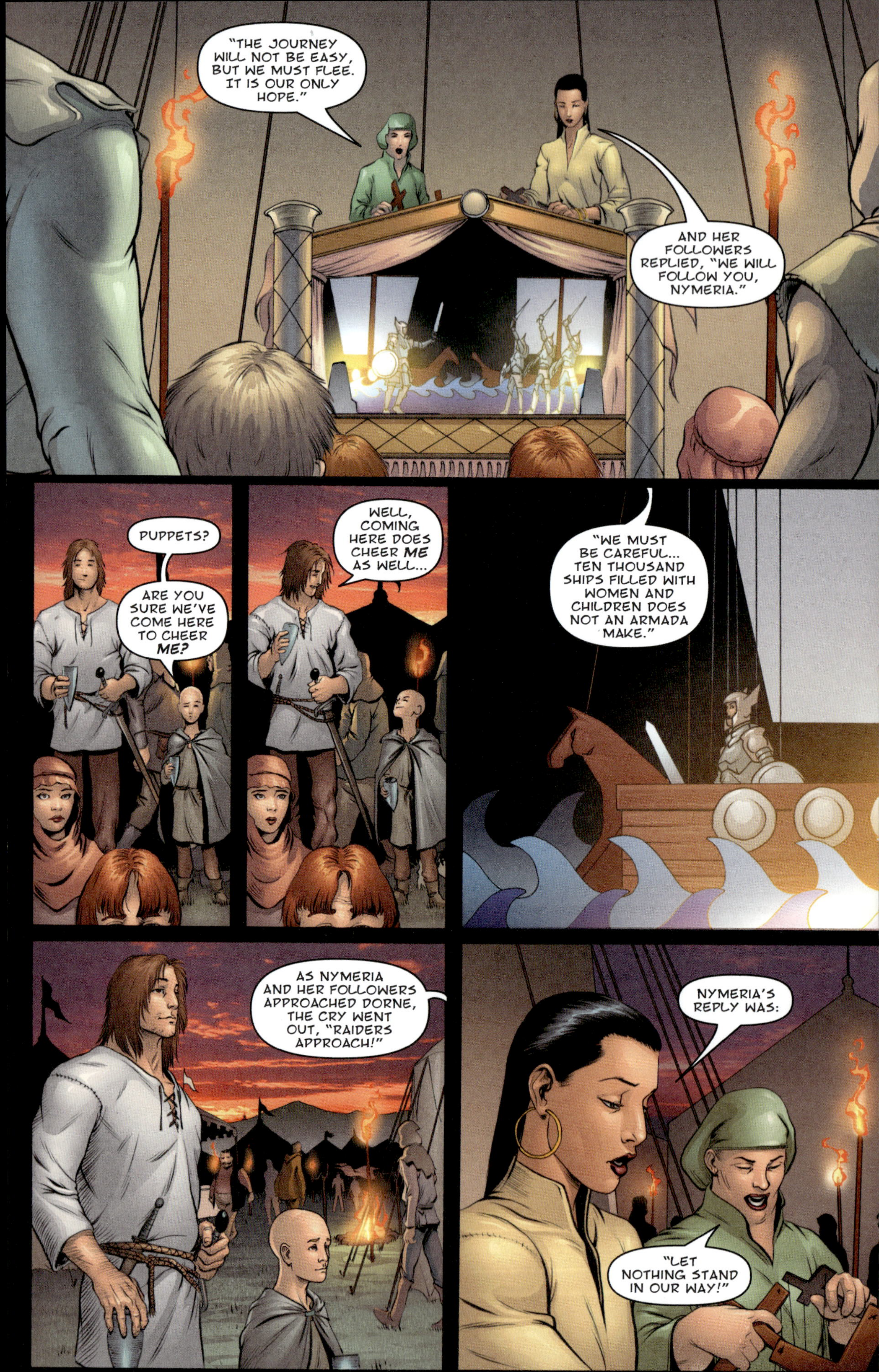
"THE JOURNEY WILL NOT BE EASY, BUT WE MUST FLEE. IT IS OUR ONLY HOPE."
AND HER FOLLOWERS REPLIED, "WE WILL FOLLOW YOU, NYMERIA."
PUPPETS?
ARE YOU SURE WE'VE COME HERE TO CHEER ME?
WELL, COMING HERE DOES CHEER ME AS WELL...
"WE MUST BE CAREFUL... TEN THOUSAND SHIPS FILLED WITH WOMEN AND CHILDREN DOES NOT AN ARMADA MAKE."
AS NYMERIA AND HER FOLLOWERS APPROACHED DORNE, THE CRY WENT OUT, "RAIDERS APPROACH!"
NYMERIA'S REPLY WAS:
"LET NOTHING STAND IN OUR WAY!"

YAY!
HOORAY!
BUT THE BATTLE WAS NOT YET OVER!
DID YOU SEE THAT?
I WANTED TO ASK THE GIRL TANSELLE IF SHE HAD FINISHED PAINTING MY SHIELD.
SHE WAS BUSY NOW; I COULD WAIT.
"LOOK!" NYMERIA'S FOLLOWERS SAID. "ANOTHER APPROACHES AND WE HAVE NOT THE SPEED TO RAM AGAIN!"
AND NYMERIA REPLIED:
"THEN WE FIGHT! WE HAVE NO OTHER CHOICE!
WAIT UNTIL SHE WAS DONE FOR THE NIGHT--
--PERHAPS SHE WOULD HAVE A THIRST THEN.
"LET NOTHING STAND IN OUR WAY!"
SER DUNCAN!
SER DUNCAN!
SER DUNCAN!
SUDDENLY, I REMEMBERED. "SER DUNCAN" WAS ME.
RAYMUN!

I SAW YOU AMONG THE SMALLFOLK TODAY, WITH THIS BOY ON YOUR SHOULDERS. THE TWO OF YOU WERE HARD TO MISS.
THE BOY IS MY SQUIRE.
EGG, THIS IS RAYMUN FOSSOWAY.
HULLO.
WELL MET, LAD.
SER DUNCAN, WHY NOT WATCH FROM THE VIEWING GALLERY? ALL KNIGHTS ARE WELCOME THERE.
I WOULD NOT HAVE WANTED AN CLOSER VIEW OF THAT LAST TILT.
I WAS AT EASE WITH SMALLFOLK AND SERVANTS; THE IDEA OF CLAIMING A PLACE AMONG THE LORDS, LADIES, AND LANDED KNIGHTS MADE ME UNCOMFORTABLE.
NOR I. LORD ASHFORD DECLARED SER HUMFREY THE VICTOR AND AWARDED HIM PRINCE AERION'S COURSER, BUT HIS LEG WAS BROKEN IN TWO PLACES AND HE WILL NOT BE ABLE TO CONTINUE.
PRINCE BAELOR SENT HIS OWN MAESTER TO TEND HIM.
WILL THERE BE ANOTHER CHAMPION IN SER HUMFREY'S PLACE?
PRINCE BAELOR SAID IT WOULD NOT BE SEEMLY TO REMOVE SER HUMFREY'S SHIELD UNDER THE CIRCUMSTANCES.
THEY WILL CONTINUE WITH FOUR CHAMPIONS IN PLACE OF FIVE.
FOUR CHAMPIONS.
LEO TYRELL, LYONEL BARATHEON, TYBOLT LANNISTER, AND PRINCE VALARR. I WOULD STAND LITTLE CHANCE AGAINST THE FIRST THREE, WHICH LEFT ONLY...
BUT A HEDGE KNIGHT COULD NOT CHALLENGE A PRINCE. VALARR WAS BAELOR BREAKSPEAR'S SON AND SECOND IN LINE TO THE IRON THRONE. HIS BLOOD WAS THE BLOOD OF AEGON THE CONQUEROR AND THE YOUNG DRAGON AND PRINCE AEMON THE DRAGONKNIGHT.
AND I WAS SOME BOY THE OLD MAN FOUND BEHIND A POT SHOP IN FLEA BOTTOM.
MY HEAD HURT JUST THINKING ABOUT IT.

WHO DOES YOUR COUSIN MEAN TO CHALLENGE?
SER TYBOLT. THEY ARE WELL MATCHED. BUT MY COUSIN KEEPS A SHARP WATCH ON EVERY TILT. SHOULD ANY MAN BE WOUNDED OR SHOW SIGNS OF WEAKNESS, STEFFON WILL BE QUICK TO KNOCK ON HIS SHIELD.
NO ONE HAS EVER ACCUSED HIM OF AN EXCESS OF CHIVALRY!
SER DUNCAN, WILL YOU JOIN ME FOR A CUP OF WINE?
I HAVE A MATTER I MUST ATTEND TO.
I COULD WAIT HERE AND BRING YOUR SHIELD WHEN THE PUPPET SHOW IS OVER.
THEY'RE GOING TO DO SYMEON STAREYES AND THEN THE DRAGON FIGHT AGAIN!
THERE, YOU SEE, YOUR MATTER IS ATTENDED TO, AND THE WINE AWAITS. HOW CAN YOU REFUSE ME?
I WAS UNCOMFORTABLE WITH THE NOTION OF ACCEPTING HOSPITALITY I COULD NOT RETURN, BUT --
-- BEREFT OF EXCUSES, I HAD NO CHOICE BUT TO FOLLOW.
THE RAIDERS SLAIN, NYMERIA PROUDLY DECLARED:
"WE HAVE FOUGHT LIKE WARRIORS ON THIS DAY!"
VERY WELL.

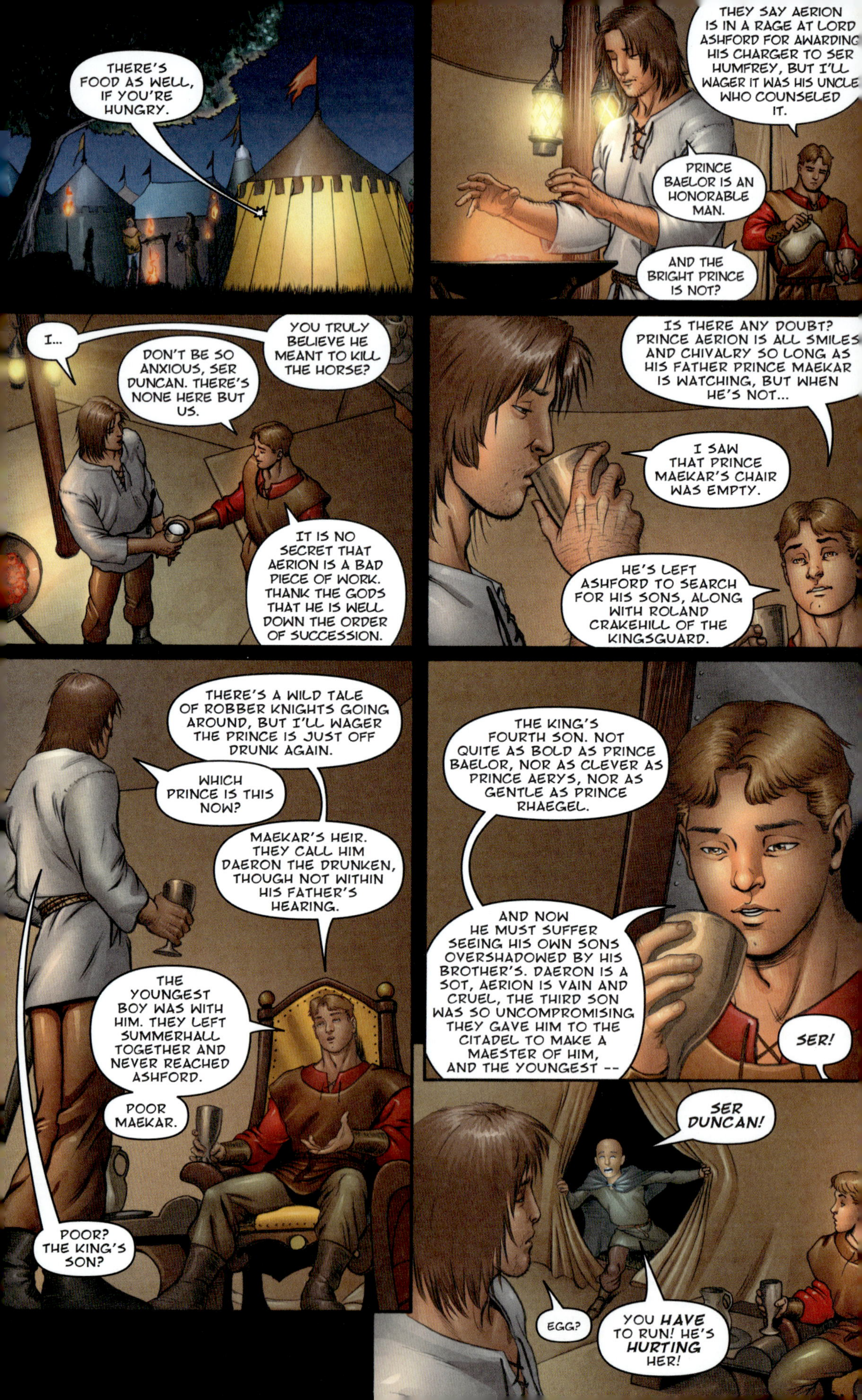
THERE'S FOOD AS WELL, IF YOU'RE HUNGRY.
THEY SAY AERION IS IN A RAGE AT LORD ASHFORD FOR AWARDING HIS CHARGER TO SER HUMFREY, BUT I'LL WAGER IT WAS HIS UNCLE WHO COUNSELED IT.
PRINCE BAELOR IS AN HONORABLE MAN.
AND THE BRIGHT PRINCE IS NOT?
YOU TRULY BELIEVE HE MEANT TO KILL THE HORSE?
I...
DON'T BE SO ANXIOUS, SER DUNCAN. THERE'S NONE HERE BUT US.
IT IS NO SECRET THAT AERION IS A BAD PIECE OF WORK. THANK THE GODS THAT HE IS WELL DOWN THE ORDER OF SUCCESSION.
IS THERE ANY DOUBT? PRINCE AERION IS ALL SMILES AND CHIVALRY SO LONG AS HIS FATHER PRINCE MAEKAR IS WATCHING, BUT WHEN HE'S NOT...
I SAW THAT PRINCE MAEKAR'S CHAIR WAS EMPTY.
HE'S LEFT ASHFORD TO SEARCH FOR HIS SONS, ALONG WITH ROLAND CRAKEHILL OF THE KINGSGUARD.
THERE'S A WILD TALE OF ROBBER KNIGHTS GOING AROUND, BUT I'LL WAGER THE PRINCE IS JUST OFF DRUNK AGAIN.
WHICH PRINCE IS THIS NOW?
MAEKAR'S HEIR. THEY CALL HIM DAERON THE DRUNKEN, THOUGH NOT WITHIN HIS FATHER'S HEARING.
THE YOUNGEST BOY WAS WITH HIM. THEY LEFT SUMMERHALL TOGETHER AND NEVER REACHED ASHFORD.
POOR MAEKAR.
POOR? THE KING'S SON?
THE KING'S FOURTH SON. NOT QUITE AS BOLD AS PRINCE BAELOR, NOR AS CLEVER AS PRINCE AERYS, NOR AS GENTLE AS PRINCE RHAEGEL.
AND NOW HE MUST SUFFER SEEING HIS OWN SONS OVERSHADOWED BY HIS BROTHER'S. DAERON IS A SOT, AERION IS VAIN AND CRUEL, THE THIRD SON WAS SO UNCOMPROMISING THEY GAVE HIM TO THE CITADEL TO MAKE A MAESTER OF HIM, AND THE YOUNGEST --
SER!
SER DUNCAN!
EGG?
YOU HAVE TO RUN! HE'S HURTING HER!

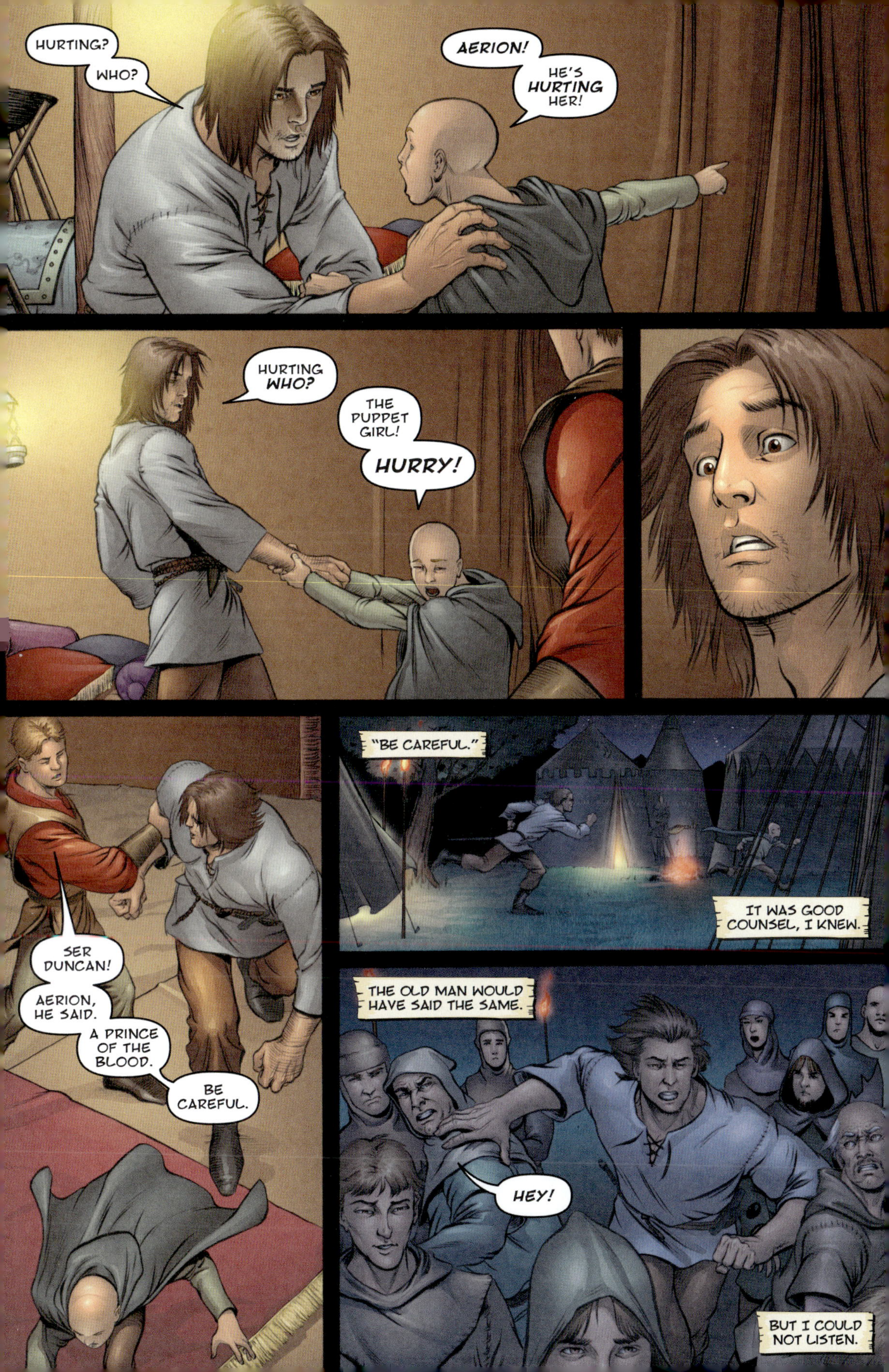
HURTING?
WHO?
AERION!
HE'S HURTING HER!
HURTING WHO?
THE PUPPET GIRL!
HURRY!
SER DUNCAN!
AERION, HE SAID.
A PRINCE OF THE BLOOD.
BE CAREFUL.
"BE CAREFUL."
IT WAS GOOD COUNSEL, I KNEW.
THE OLD MAN WOULD HAVE SAID THE SAME.
HEY!
BUT I COULD NOT LISTEN.

NO! PLEASE!
PLEA--
CRACK
ARRRGGH

PLEASE DON'T!

NO...
N-NO...
MY SWORD AND DAGGER WERE FORGOTTEN --
--ALONG WITH EVERYTHING THE OLD MAN HAD EVER TAUGHT ME.
KRAK

UFF
I MIGHT HAVE KICKED HIM TO DEATH RIGHT THEN AND THERE, BUT...

AGH
HUNH
GOT 'IM!

=UGHNH=
NOW, LET'S GET HIM!
HE'S LIKE AN AUROCHS!
ARRRRH!
HOLD HIM!
YOU'VE LOOSENED ONE OF MY TEETH...

...SO WE'LL START BY BREAKING ALL OF YOURS.
YOU LOOK FAMILIAR.
YOU TOOK ME FOR A STABLEBOY.
I RECALL. YOU REFUSED TO TAKE MY HORSE.
WHY DID YOU THROW YOUR LIFE AWAY? FOR THIS WHORE? SHE'S SCARCELY WORTH IT. A TRAITOR.
THE DRAGON OUGHT NEVER LOSE.
HE WAS MAD, BUT HE WAS STILL A PRINCE'S SON AND HE MEANT TO KILL ME.
I MIGHT HAVE PRAYED THEN, IF I HAD KNOWN A PRAYER ALL THE WAY THROUGH, BUT THERE WAS NO TIME.
THERE WAS HARDLY EVEN TIME TO BE AFRAID.
NOTHING MORE TO SAY? YOU BORE ME, SER.
GET A HAMMER AND BREAK ALL HIS TEETH OUT, WATE, AND THEN LET'S CUT HIM OPEN AND SHOW HIM THE COLOR OF HIS ENTRAILS.
NO!
DON'T HURT HIM!
GODS BE GOOD, THE BOY, THE BRAVE FOOLISH BOY.
HOLD YOUR TONGUE, YOU STUPID BOY!
RUN AWAY! THEY'LL HURT YOU!
NO THEY WON'T.

IF THEY DO, THEY WILL ANSWER TO MY FATHER.
AND MY UNCLE AS WELL.
LET GO OF HIM, I SAID!
WATE! YORKEL! YOU KNOW ME! DO AS I SAY!
IMPUDENT LITTLE WRETCH.
WHAT HAPPENED TO YOUR HAIR?
I CUT IT OFF, BROTHER.
I DIDN'T WANT TO LOOK LIKE YOU.

THE SECOND DAY OF THE TOURNEY WAS OVERCAST, WITH A GUSTY WIND BLOWING IN FROM THE WEST.
THE CROWDS WOULD BE LESS, MAKING IT MUCH EASIER TO FIND A SPOT NEAR THE FENCE TO SEE THE JOUSTING UP CLOSE...
EGG MIGHT HAVE SAT ON THE RAIL WHILE I STOOD BEHIND HIM.
INSTEAD, EGG WOULD HAVE A SEAT IN THE VIEWING BOX, WHILE MY VIEW WAS LIMITED TO THE FOUR WALLS OF THE TOWER CELL WHERE LORD ASHFORD'S MEN HAD CONFINED ME.
THEY HAD TAKEN EVERYTHING -- MY HEMPEN SWORD BELT, MY SWORD AND DAGGER, EVEN MY SILVER.
I HOPED EGG OR RAYMUN WOULD REMEMBER CHESTNUT AND THUNDER.
EGG...
MY SQUIRE, A POOR LAD PLUCKED FROM THE STREETS OF KING'S LANDING. HAD EVER A KNIGHT BEEN MADE SUCH A FOOL?
"DUNK THE LUNK, THICK AS A CASTLE WALL AND SLOW AS AN AUROCHS."
MY WINDOW FACED THE WRONG DIRECTION, BUT I COULD HEAR THE JOUSTING.
THE FAINT HOOFBEATS. TH HORNS. THE ROA OF THE CROWD
AND ONCE IN A WHILE, THE CLASH OF SWORDS OR SNAP OF A LANCE.
I WINCED WHENEVER I HEARD THAT LAS IT REMINDED ME OF THE NOISE TANSELLE'S FINGER HAD MAD WHEN...

PUSHED THAT
OUGHT AWAY.
ANOTHER THOUGHT TOOK ITS PLACE, ACCOMPANIED BY THE SAME SOUNDS -- DISTANT HOOFBEATS, THE ROAR OF CROWDS, THE CLAMOR OF STEEL AGAINST STEEL, HORNS...
YOU FOUGHT FIERCELY, SER, BUT IT IS THE LORD'S MEN WHO WILL TAKE ALL THE GLORY WHEN THEY TELL OF THIS BATTLE.
YES.
BUT IF YOU THINK THAT MATTERS YOU'RE THICKER THAN I THOUGHT. HAVE YOU LEARNED NOTHING FROM ME?
A HEDGE KNIGHT IS THE TRUEST KIND OF KNIGHT, DUNK.
OTHER KNIGHTS SERVE THE LORDS WHO KEEP THEM, OR FROM WHOM THEY HOLD THEIR LANDS, BUT WE SERVE WHERE WE WILL, FOR MEN WHOSE CAUSES WE BELIEVE IN.
EVERY KNIGHT SWEARS TO PROTECT THE WEAK AND INNOCENT, BUT WE KEEP THE VOW THE BEST, I THINK.
YES, SER.
QUEER HOW STRONG THAT MEMORY SEEMED.
I HAD QUITE FORGOTTEN THOSE WORDS. AND PERHAPS, THE OLD MAN HAD AS WELL, TOWARD THE END.
MORNING TURNED TO AFTERNOON. AFTERNOON GAVE WAY TO THE GATHERING DARK OF EVENING.

LEAVE THE LAMP AND FOOD AND GO.
THERE'S NO KNIFE. DID THEY THINK I WOULD STAB YOU?
THEY DIDN'T TELL ME WHAT THEY THOUGHT.
MY UNCLE SAYS I MUST HUMBLY BEG YOUR FORGIVENESS FOR DECEIVING YOU.
YOUR UNCLE.
THAT WOULD BE PRINCE BAELOR.
I NEVER MEANT TO LIE.
BUT YOU DID.
ABOUT EVERYTHING. STARTING WITH YOUR NAME. I NEVER HEARD OF A PRINCE EGG.
IT'S SHORT FOR AEGON.
AEGON. OF COURSE. LIKE AEGON THE DRAGON. HOW MANY AEGONS HAVE BEEN KING?
FOUR.
FOUR AEGONS.

WHY DID YOU DO IT?
WAS IT SOME JAPE, TO MAKE A FOOL OF THE STUPID HEDGE KNIGHT?
NO.
I WAS SUPPOSED TO SQUIRE FOR DAERON, MY OLDEST BROTHER, BUT HE DIDN'T WANT TO RIDE IN THE TOURNEY, SO WE STOLE AWAY FROM OUR ESCORT.
IT WAS HIM WHO SHAVED MY HEAD. DAERON HAS COMMON HAIR, PALE BROWN, BUT MINE IS LIKE AERION'S AND MY FATHER'S.
THE BLOOD OF DRAGON.
SILVER-GOLD HAIR AND PURPLE EYES, EVERYONE KNOWS THAT.
"THICK AS A CASTLE WALL."
DAERON MEANT FOR US TO HIDE, BUT THEN YOU TOOK ME FOR A STABLEBOY, AND...
I DIDN'T CARE IF DAERON FOUGHT OR NOT, BUT I WANTED TO BE SOMEBODY'S SQUIRE.
I'M SORRY, SER, I TRULY AM.
I KNEW WHAT IT WAS TO WANT SOMETHING SO BADLY THAT YOU WOULD TELL A MONSTROUS LIE JUST TO GET NEAR IT.
I THOUGHT YOU WERE LIKE ME.
MIGHT BE YOU ARE, ONLY NOT THE WAY I THOUGHT.
WE'RE BOTH FROM KING'S LANDING STILL.
YES, YOU FROM THE TOP OF AEGON'S HILL AND ME FROM THE BOTTOM.
THAT'S NOT SO FAR, SER.
DO I NEED TO CALL YOU M'LORD OR OUR GRACE OR SOMETHING?
AT COURT, BUT OTHER TIMES YOU CAN KEEP CALLING ME EGG, SER.
WHAT WILL THEY DO WITH ME, EGG?
MY UNCLE WANTS TO SEE YOU.
AFTER YOU'RE DONE EATING, SER.
I'M DONE NOW, THEN. I'VE ALREADY KICKED ONE PRINCE IN THE MOUTH, I DON'T MEAN TO KEEP ANOTHER WAITING.

LORD ASHFORD HAD TURNED HIS CHAMBERS OVER TO PRINCE BAELOR FOR THE DURATION OF HIS STAY, SO IT THERE THAT EGG -- AEGON -- CONDUCTED ME.
RISE.
WOULD YOU CARE FOR WINE?
POUR SER DUNCAN A CUP OF THE SWEET DORNISH RED, AEGON.
AS IT PLEASE YOU, YOUR GRACE.
TRY NOT TO SPILL IT ON HIM, YOU'VE DONE HIM SUFFICIENT ILL ALREADY.
THE BOY WON'T SPILL, YOUR GRACE.
HE'S A GOOD BOY. A GOOD SQUIRE. AND HE MEANT NO HARM TO ME, I KNOW.
ONE NEED NOT INTEND HARM TO DO IT.
AEGON SHOULD HAVE COME TO ME WHEN HE SAW WHAT HIS BROTHER WAS DOING. INSTEAD HE RAN TO YOU. THAT WAS NO KINDNESS.
WHAT YOU DID, SER... WELL, I MIGHT HAVE DONE THE SAME THING, BUT I AM PRINCE OF THE REALM, NOT A HEDGE KNIGHT.
IT IS NEVER WISE TO STRIKE A KING'S GRANDSON IN ANGER, NO MATTER THE CAUSE.
I HATE AERION.
AND I HAD TO RUN FOR SER DUNCAN, UNCLE, THE CASTLE WAS TOO FAR.
AERION IS YOUR BROTHER, AND THE SEPTONS SAY WE MUST LOVE OUR BROTHERS.
AEGON, LEAVE US NOW, I WOULD SPEAK WITH SER DUNCAN PRIVATELY.
AS YOU WILL, YOUR GRACE.

SER DUNCAN, LET ME ASK YOU THIS--
--HOW GOOD OF A KNIGHT ARE YOU, TRULY?
HOW SKILLED AT ARMS?
SER ARLAN TAUGHT ME SWORD AND SHIELD, AND HOW TO TILT AT RINGS AND QUINTAINS.
MY BROTHER MAEKAR FOUND HIS SON DAERON DRUNK IN AN INN A DAY'S RIDE TO THE SOUTH.
MAEKAR HOPED THAT HIS SONS MIGHT OUTSHINE MINE IN THIS TOURNEY. INSTEAD DAERON AND AERION HAVE BOTH SHAMED HIM.
HE IS ANGRY AND MUST NEEDS HAVE A TARGET FOR HIS WRATH.
HE HAS CHOSEN YOU.
ME?
AERION HAS ALREADY FILLED HIS FATHER'S EAR ABOUT THE "HIGH TREASON" OF THE PUPPETEERS. THE DRAGON IS THE SIGIL OF THE ROYAL HOUSE.
THE PORTRAYAL OF ONE BEING SLAIN, AERION CLAIMS, WAS A VEILED ATTACK ON HOUSE TARGARYEN.
AND DAERON HAS TOLD MY BROTHER THAT A HUGE ROBBER KNIGHT MADE OFF WITH AEGON AND HE SPENT ALL THESE DAYS PURSUING THE KNIGHT HITHER AND YON, TO WIN BACK HIS BROTHER.
I FEAR YOU HAVE BEEN CAST AS THIS ROBBER KNIGHT, SER.
BUT EGG WILL TELL HIM THE TRUTH.
AEGON, I MEAN.
HE WILL.
BUT THE BOY HAS BEEN KNOWN TO LIE, AS YOU CAN RECALL. WHICH SON WILL MY BROTHER BELIEVE?
WHATEVER MY BROTHER BELIEVES OR FAILS TO BELIEVE, ONE TRUTH IS BEYOND DISPUTE.
YOU LAID HANDS UPON THE BLOOD OF THE DRAGON AND FOR THAT OFFENSE, YOU MUST BE PUNISHED.
PUNISHED?

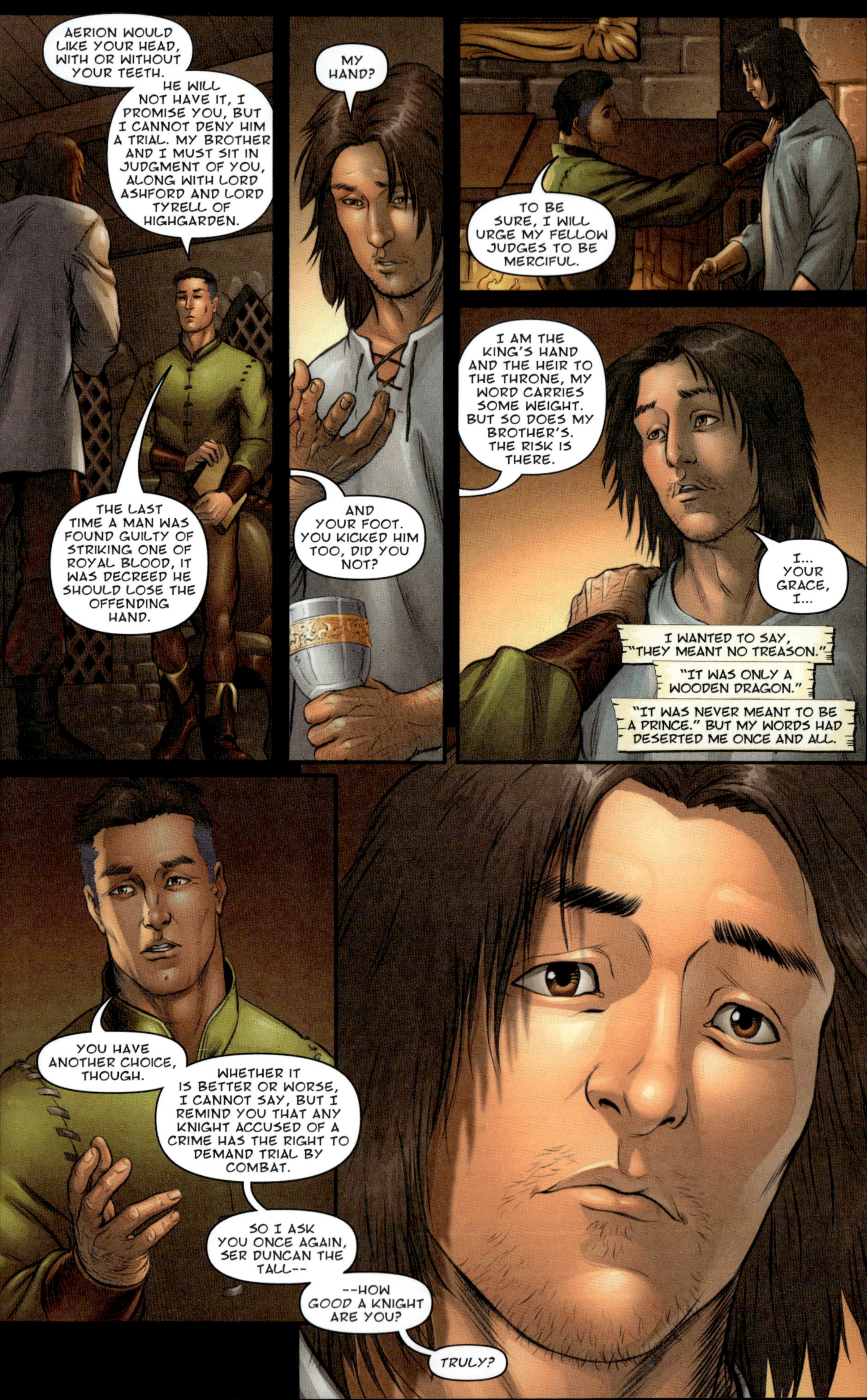
AERION WOULD LIKE YOUR HEAD, WITH OR WITHOUT YOUR TEETH.
HE WILL NOT HAVE IT, I PROMISE YOU, BUT I CANNOT DENY HIM A TRIAL. MY BROTHER AND I MUST SIT IN JUDGMENT OF YOU, ALONG WITH LORD ASHFORD AND LORD TYRELL OF HIGHGARDEN.
THE LAST TIME A MAN WAS FOUND GUILTY OF STRIKING ONE OF ROYAL BLOOD, IT WAS DECREED HE SHOULD LOSE THE OFFENDING HAND.
MY HAND?
AND YOUR FOOT. YOU KICKED HIM TOO, DID YOU NOT?
TO BE SURE, I WILL URGE MY FELLOW JUDGES TO BE MERCIFUL.
I AM THE KING'S HAND AND THE HEIR TO THE THRONE, MY WORD CARRIES SOME WEIGHT. BUT SO DOES MY BROTHER'S. THE RISK IS THERE.
I... YOUR GRACE, I...
I WANTED TO SAY, "THEY MEANT NO TREASON."
"IT WAS ONLY A WOODEN DRAGON."
"IT WAS NEVER MEANT TO BE A PRINCE." BUT MY WORDS HAD DESERTED ME ONCE AND ALL.
YOU HAVE ANOTHER CHOICE, THOUGH.
WHETHER IT IS BETTER OR WORSE, I CANNOT SAY, BUT I REMIND YOU THAT ANY KNIGHT ACCUSED OF A CRIME HAS THE RIGHT TO DEMAND TRIAL BY COMBAT.
SO I ASK YOU ONCE AGAIN, SER DUNCAN THE TALL--
--HOW GOOD A KNIGHT ARE YOU?
TRULY?

ISSUE FIVE
COVER A
MIKE S. MILLER

ISSUE FIVE
COVER B
TED NASMITH

A TRIAL OF SEVEN.
THAT IS MY RIGHT, I DO BELIEVE.
STANDING BEFORE THE MEN THAT WERE TO JUDGE ME, PRINCE AERION, MY ACCUSER, WAS ALL SMILES.
PRINCE BAELOR DRUMMED HIS FINGERS ON THE TABLE, FROWNING. LORD ASHFORD NODDED SLOWLY. LORD TYRELL OF HIGHGARDEN, ASHFORD'S LIEGE LORD, WAITED SILENTLY AS BAELOR'S BROTHER PRINCE MAEKAR LEANED FORWARD, DEMANDING OF HIS SON:
WHY?
ARE YOU AFRAID TO FACE THIS HEDGE KNIGHT ALONE, AND LET THE GODS DECIDE THE TRUTH OF YOUR ACCUSATIONS?
AFRAID?

OF SUCH AS THIS?
DON'T BE ABSURD, FATHER. MY THOUGHT IS FOR MY BELOVED BROTHER.
DAERON HAS BEEN WRONGED BY THIS SER DUNCAN AS WELL, AND HAS FIRST CLAIM TO HIS BLOOD. A TRIAL OF SEVEN ALLOWS BOTH OF US TO FACE HIM.
DO ME NO FAVORS, BROTHER.
I AM CONTENT TO CHEER YOU ON AS YOU SLAY THE ROGUE.
YOU ARE TOO KIND, SWEET BROTHER, BUT IT WOUL BE SELFISH OF ME TO DENY YOU THE RIGHT T PROVE THE TRUTH OF YOUR WORDS AT THE HAZARD OF YOUR BODY.
I MUST INSIST UPO A TRIAL BY SEVEN.
YOUR GRACE, MY LORDS.
I DO NOT UNDERSTAND.
WHAT IS THIS TRIAL OF SEVEN?
IT IS AN ANCIENT, SELDOM INVOKED FORM OF TRIAL BY COMBAT.
IT CAME ACROSS THE NARROW SEA WITH THE ANDALS AND THEIR SEVEN GODS. THEY BELIEVED THAT IF SEVEN CHAMPIONS FOUGHT ON EACH SIDE, THE GODS, BEING THUS HONORED, WOULD BE MORE LIKE TO TAKE A HAND AND SEE THAT A JUST RESULT WAS ACHIEVED.
OR MAYHAP THEY SIMPLY HAD A TASTE FOR SWORDPLAY. REGARDLESS, SER AERION IS WITHIN HIS RIGHTS. A TRIAL OF SEVEN IT MUST BE.
I MUST FIGHT **SEVEN MEN**, THEN?
DON'T PLAY THE FOOL, IT WILL NOT SERVE. YOU MUST NEEDS FIND SIX OTHER KNIGHTS TO FIGHT BESIDE YOU.
YOUR GRACES, MY LORDS.
WHAT IF NO ONE WILL TAKE MY PART?

IF A CAUSE IS JUST, GOOD MEN WILL FIGHT FOR IT.
IF YOU CAN FIND NO CHAMPIONS, SER, IT WILL BE BECAUSE YOU ARE GUILTY.
COULD ANYTHING BE MORE CLEAR?
I HAD NEVER FELT SO ALONE AS I DID WHEN I WALKED OUT THE GATES OF ASHFORD CASTLE AND HEARD THE PORTCULLIS COME DOWN BEHIND ME.
SIX KNIGHTS?
THEY MIGHT AS WELL HAVE TOLD ME TO FIND SIX THOUSAND. I HAD NO BROTHERS, NO COUSINS, NO OLD COMRADES WHO HAD STOOD BESIDE ME IN BATTLE.
WHY WOULD SIX KNIGHTS RISK THEIR OWN LIVES TO DEFEND A HEDGE KNIGHT AGAINST TWO ROYAL PRINCELINGS?
THE NIGHT WAS HALF GONE, I GUESSED.
DAWN WOULD BE ON ME IN A FEW HOURS.
AND WITH DAWN CAME DEATH.
I WONDERED IF THEY EXPECTED ME TO FLEE.
THAT WOULD BE THE END OF MY KNIGHTHOOD, TO BE SURE; I WOULD BE NO MORE THAN AN OUTLAW HENCEFORTH, UNTIL THE DAY SOME LORD TOOK ME AND STRUCK OFF MY HEAD.

BETTER TO DIE A KNIGHT THAN LIVE LIKE THAT.
I HEARD THE SOFT MOANS AND CRIES OF PLEASURE COMING FROM ONE TENT AND I WONDERED IF I WOULD DIE WITHOUT EVER HAVING KNOWN A MAID.
THEN...
NEEEIGH
THUNDER?
THERE HE WAS, TIED UP WITH CHESTNUT OUTSIDE A ROUND PAVILION LIT FROM WITHIN BY A VAGUE GOLDEN GLOW.
ON ITS CENTER POLE, THE BANNER HUNG SODDEN, BUT I COULD STILL MAKE OUT THE DARK CURVE OF THE FOSSOWAY APPLE.
IT LOOKED LIKE HOPE.

A TRIAL BY COMBAT.
GODS BE GOOD, DUNCAN, THAT MEANS LANCES OF WAR, MORNINGSTARS, BATTLE-AXES...
THE SWORDS *WON'T* BE BLUNTED, DO YOU UNDERSTAND THAT?
YOU NEED NOT FEAR, COUSIN, THIS IS *KNIGHTLY* COMBAT.
AS YOU ARE NO KNIGHT, YOUR SKIN IS NOT AT RISK.
RAYMUN THE RELUCTANT.
SER DUNCAN, YOU HAVE ONE FOSSOWAY AT LEAST. THE *RIPE* ONE.
I SAW WHAT AERION DID TO THOSE PUPPETEERS. I AM FOR YOU.
AND I!
I ONLY MEANT --
WHO ELSE FIGHTS FOR US, SER DUNCAN?
I KNOW NO ONE ELSE.
WELL, EXCEPT FOR SER MANFRED DONDARRION.
HE WOULDN'T EVEN VOUCH THAT I WAS A KNIGHT, HE'LL NEVER RISK HIS LIFE FOR ME.
THEN WE NEED FIVE MORE GOOD MEN. FORTUNATELY, I HAVE MORE THAN FIVE FRIENDS.
LEO LONGTHORN, THE LAUGHING STORM, LORD CARON, THE LANNISTERS, SER OTHO BRACKEN... AYE, THE BLACKWOODS AS WELL, THOUGH YOU WILL NEVER GET BLACKWOOD AND BRACKEN ON THE SAME SIDE OF A MELEE.
I SHALL GO AND SPEAK WITH SOME OF THEM.

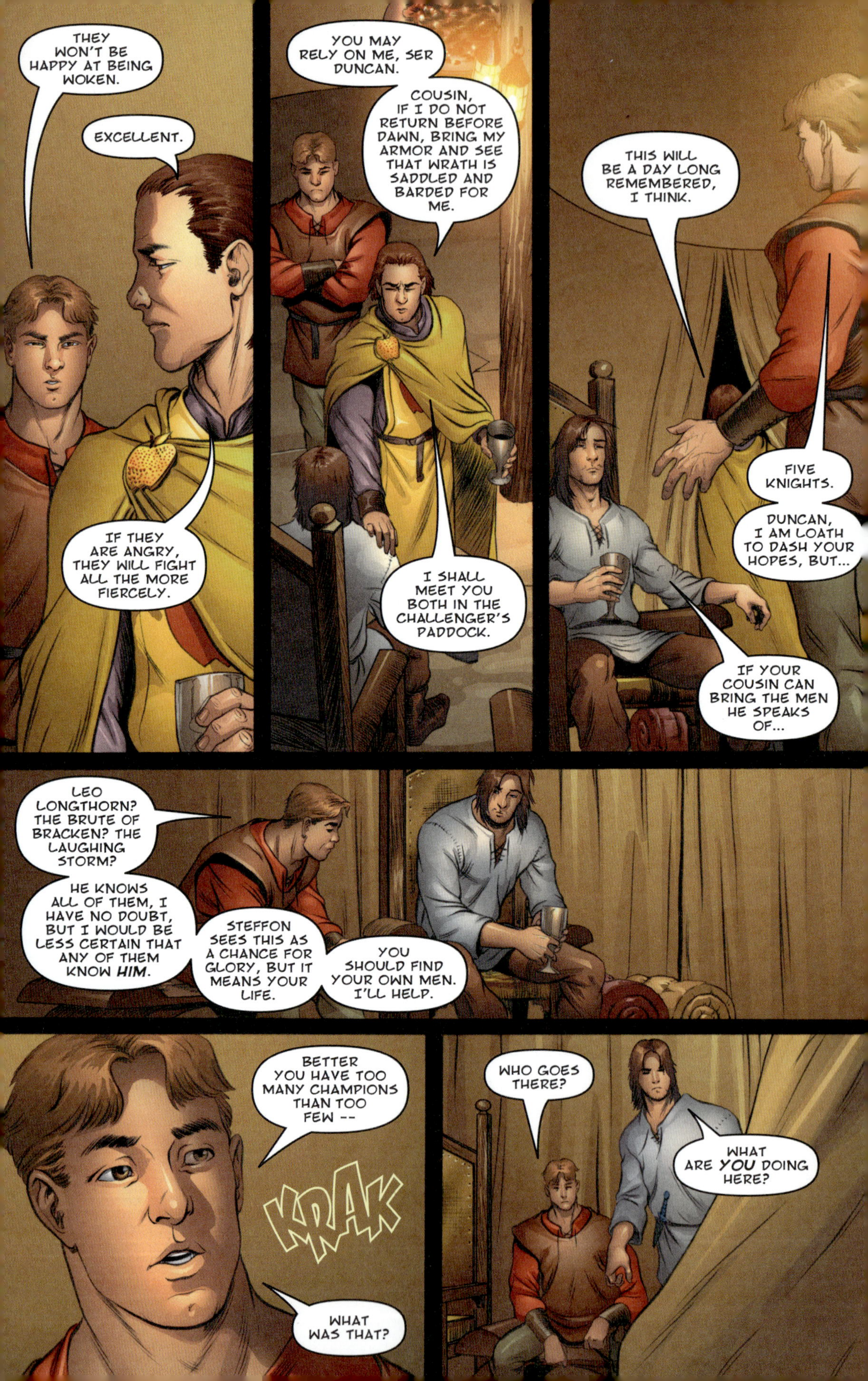
THEY WON'T BE HAPPY AT BEING WOKEN.
EXCELLENT.
IF THEY ARE ANGRY, THEY WILL FIGHT ALL THE MORE FIERCELY.
YOU MAY RELY ON ME, SER DUNCAN.
COUSIN, IF I DO NOT RETURN BEFORE DAWN, BRING MY ARMOR AND SEE THAT WRATH IS SADDLED AND BARDED FOR ME.
I SHALL MEET YOU BOTH IN THE CHALLENGER'S PADDOCK.
THIS WILL BE A DAY LONG REMEMBERED, I THINK.
FIVE KNIGHTS.
DUNCAN, I AM LOATH TO DASH YOUR HOPES, BUT...
IF YOUR COUSIN CAN BRING THE MEN HE SPEAKS OF...
LEO LONGTHORN? THE BRUTE OF BRACKEN? THE LAUGHING STORM?
HE KNOWS ALL OF THEM, I HAVE NO DOUBT, BUT I WOULD BE LESS CERTAIN THAT ANY OF THEM KNOW *HIM*.
STEFFON SEES THIS AS A CHANCE FOR GLORY, BUT IT MEANS YOUR LIFE.
YOU SHOULD FIND YOUR OWN MEN. I'LL HELP.
BETTER YOU HAVE TOO MANY CHAMPIONS THAN TOO FEW --
KRAK
WHAT WAS THAT?
WHO GOES THERE?
WHAT ARE *YOU* DOING HERE?

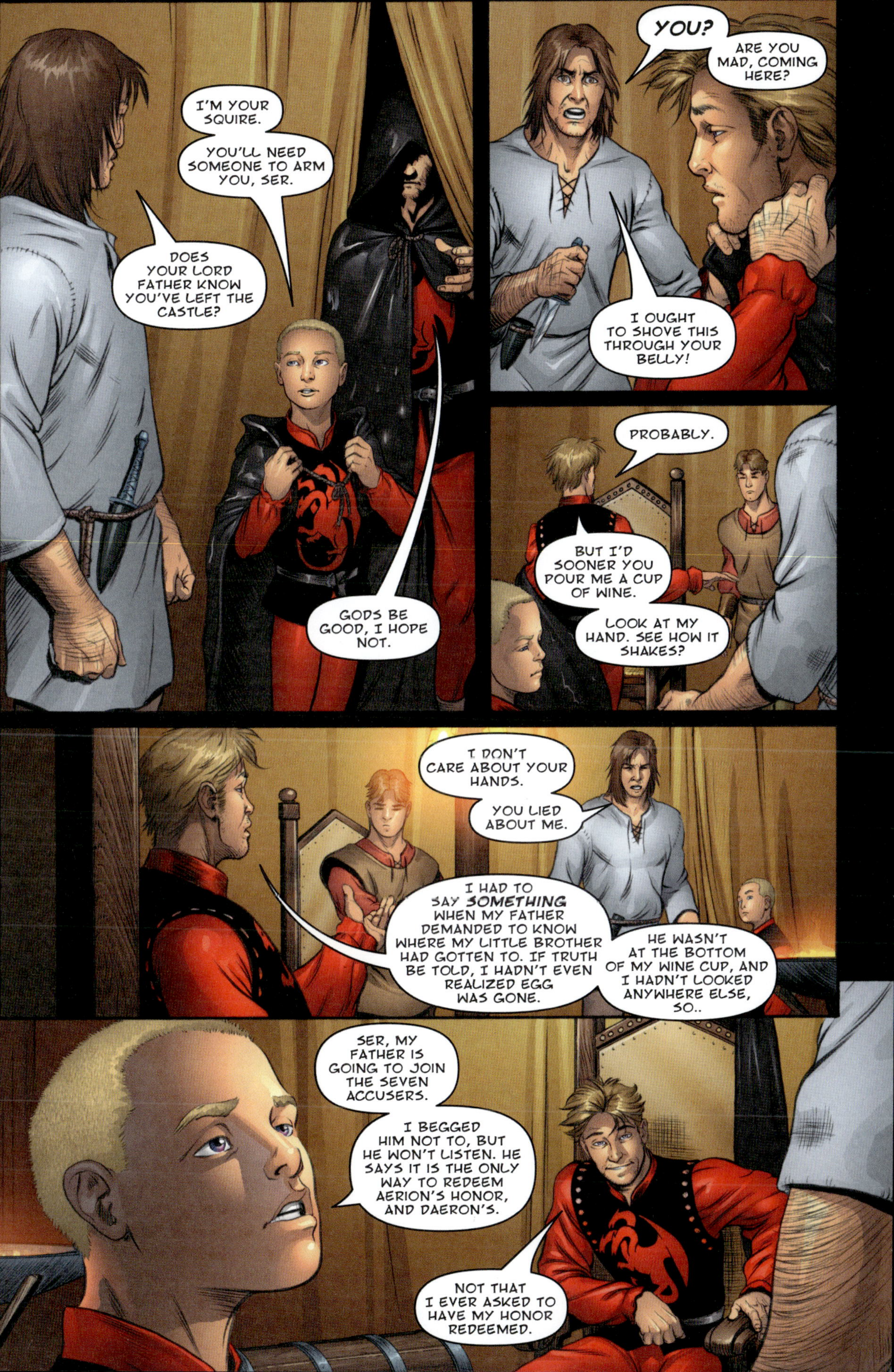
I'M YOUR SQUIRE.
YOU'LL NEED SOMEONE TO ARM YOU, SER.
DOES YOUR LORD FATHER KNOW YOU'VE LEFT THE CASTLE?
GODS BE GOOD, I HOPE NOT.
YOU?
ARE YOU MAD, COMING HERE?
I OUGHT TO SHOVE THIS THROUGH YOUR BELLY!
PROBABLY.
BUT I'D SOONER YOU POUR ME A CUP OF WINE.
LOOK AT MY HAND. SEE HOW IT SHAKES?
I DON'T CARE ABOUT YOUR HANDS.
YOU LIED ABOUT ME.
I HAD TO SAY SOMETHING WHEN MY FATHER DEMANDED TO KNOW WHERE MY LITTLE BROTHER HAD GOTTEN TO. IF TRUTH BE TOLD, I HADN'T EVEN REALIZED EGG WAS GONE.
HE WASN'T AT THE BOTTOM OF MY WINE CUP, AND I HADN'T LOOKED ANYWHERE ELSE, SO..
SER, MY FATHER IS GOING TO JOIN THE SEVEN ACCUSERS.
I BEGGED HIM NOT TO, BUT HE WON'T LISTEN. HE SAYS IT IS THE ONLY WAY TO REDEEM AERION'S HONOR, AND DAERON'S.
NOT THAT I EVER ASKED TO HAVE MY HONOR REDEEMED.

WHOEVER HAS IT CAN KEEP IT, SO FAR AS I'M CONCERNED.
STILL, HERE WE ARE. SER DUNCAN, YOU HAVE LITTLE TO FEAR FROM ME. THE ONLY THING I LIKE LESS THAN HORSES ARE SWORDS.
HEAVY THINGS, AND BEASTLY SHARP.
I'LL DO MY BEST TO LOOK GALLANT IN THE FIRST CHARGE, BUT AFTER THAT... WELL, PERHAPS YOU COULD STRIKE ME A NICE BLOW TO THE SIDE OF MY HELM.
MAKE IT RING, BUT NOT TOO LOUD, IF YOU TAKE MY MEANING.
MY BROTHERS HAVE MY MEASURE WHEN IT COMES TO FIGHTING AND DANCING AND THINKING AND READING BOOKS...
...BUT NONE OF THEM IS HALF MY EQUAL AT LYING INSENSIBLE IN THE MUD.
WAS THE PRINCELING TRYING TO PLAY ME FOR A FOOL?
WHY DID YOU COME?
TO WARN YOU OF WHAT YOU FACE.
MY FATHER HAS COMMANDED THE KINGSGUARD TO FIGHT WITH HIM.
THE KINGSGUARD?
WELL, THE THREE WHO ARE HERE.
THANK THE GODS UNCLE BAELOR LEFT THE OTHER FOUR AT KING'S LANDING WITH OUR ROYAL GRANDFATHER.
THEY HAVE SMALL CHOICE IN THE MATTER. THEY ARE SWORN TO PROTECT THE LIVES OF THE KING AND ROYAL FAMILY, AND MY BROTHERS AND I ARE BLOOD OF THE DRAGON, GODS HELP US.
THAT MAKES SIX.
WHO IS THE SEVENTH MAN?

AERION WILL FIND SOMEONE. IF NEED BE, HE WILL BUY A CHAMPION. HE HAS NO LACK OF GOLD.
WHO DO YOU HAVE?
RAYMUN'S COUSIN, SER STEFFON.
ONLY ONE?
SER STEFFON HAS GONE TO SOME OF HIS FRIENDS.
I CAN BRING PEOPLE.
KNIGHTS.
I CAN.
EGG, I WILL BE FIGHTING YOUR OWN BROTHERS.
YOU WON'T HURT DAERON, THOUGH. HE TOLD YOU HE'D FALL DOWN.
AND AERION... I REMEMBER, WHEN I WAS LITTLE, HE USED TO COME INTO MY BEDCHAMBER AT NIGHT AND PUT HIS KNIFE BETWEEN MY LEGS.
HE HAD TOO MANY BROTHERS, HE'D SAY, MAYBE ONE NIGHT HE'D MAKE ME HIS SISTER, THEN HE COULD MARRY ME.
HE THREW MY CAT IN THE WELL TOO. HE SAID HE DIDN'T, BUT HE ALWAYS LIES.
EGG HAS THE TRUTH OF IT. AERION'S QUITE THE MONSTER. HE THINKS HE'S A DRAGON IN HUMAN FORM, YOU KNOW.
THAT'S WHY HE WAS SO WROTH AT THAT PUPPET SHOW.
A PITY HE WASN'T BORN A FOSSOWAY, THEN HE'D THINK HIMSELF AN APPLE AND WE'D ALL BE A DEAL SAFER, BUT THERE YOU ARE.
I MUST STEAL BACK TO THE CASTLE BEFORE MY FATHER WONDERS WHY I'M TAKING SO LONG TO SHARPEN MY SWORD, BUT BEFORE I GO, I WOULD LIKE A PRIVATE WORD, SER DUNCAN.
WILL YOU WALK WITH ME?
AS YOU WISH, YOUR GRACE.
I NEED TO GET MY SHIELD TOO.
EGG AND I WILL LOOK FOR KNIGHTS.

I DREAMED OF YOU.
YOU SAID THAT AT THE INN.
DID I? WELL, IT'S SO. MY DREAMS ARE NOT LIKE YOURS, SER DUNCAN.
MINE ARE TRUE.
THEY FRIGHTEN ME.
YOU FRIGHTEN ME.
"I DREAMED OF YOU AND A DEAD DRAGON.
"A GREAT BEAST, HUGE, WITH WINGS SO LARGE THEY COULD COVER THIS MEADOW.
"IT HAD FALLEN ON TOP OF YOU...

"...BUT YOU WERE ALIVE AND THE DRAGON WAS DEAD."
DID I KILL IT?
THAT I COULD NOT SAY.

WE WERE MASTERS OF THE DRAGONS ONCE, WE TARGARYENS. NOW THEY ARE ALL GONE, BUT WE REMAIN.
I DON'T CARE TO DIE TODAY. THE GODS ALONE KNOW WHY, BUT I DON'T.
SO DO ME A KINDNESS IF YOU WOULD, AND MAKE CERTAIN IT IS MY BROTHER AERION YOU SLAY.
I DON'T CARE TO DIE EITHER.
WELL, I SHAN'T KILL YOU, SER.
I'LL WITHDRAW MY ACCUSATION AS WELL, BUT IT WON'T SERVE UNLESS AERION WITHDRAWS HIS.
IT MAY BE THAT I'VE KILLED YOU WITH MY LIE. IF SO, I AM SORRY.
I'M DOOMED TO SOME HELL, I KNOW.
LIKELY ONE WITHOUT WINE.
THE MERCHANTS HAD DRAWN UP THEIR WAGONS ON THE WESTERN VERGE OF THE MEADOW.
GONE.
I HAD FEARED THEY MIGHT BE.
I WOULD FLEE AS WELL, IF I WERE NOT THICK AS A CASTLE WALL.
I WONDERED WHAT I WOULD DO FOR A SHIELD NOW.
I HAD THE SILVER TO BUY ONE, IF I COULD FIND ONE FOR SALE.
SER DUNCAN.

IF YOU ARE COME FOR YOUR SHIELD, SHE LEFT IT HERE WITH ME.
TWO HANDS AND TWO FEET, I COUNT.
SO, IT'S TO BE TRIAL BY COMBAT, IS IT?
A TRIAL OF SEVEN. HOW DID YOU KNOW?
WELL, THEY MIGHT HAVE KISSED YOU AND MADE YOU LORD, BUT IT DIDN'T SEEM LIKELY, AND IF IT WENT T'OTHER WAY, YOU'D BE MISSING SOME PARTS.
NOW FOLLOW ME.
WHERE DID SHE GO?
THEY MAKE FOR DORNE. THE GIRL'S UNCLE, NOW THERE'S A WISE MAN.
WELL GONE IS WELL FORGOT. STAY AND BE SEEN, AND BELIKE THE DRAGON REMEMBERS.
BESIDES, HE DID NOT THINK SHE OUGHT SEE YOU DIE.
YOUR RIM WAS OLD CHEAP STEEL, BRITTLE AND RUSTED.
I'VE MADE YOU A NEW ONE, TWICE AS THICK, AND PUT SOME BANDS ACROSS THE BACK.
IT WILL BE HEAVIER NOW, BUT STRONGER TOO.
THE GIRL DID THE PAINT.

SHE HAD MADE A BETTER JOB OF IT THAN I COULD HAVE HOPED FOR.
EVEN BY LANTERN LIGHT, THE SUNSET COLORS WERE RICH AND BRIGHT, THE TREE STRONG AND NOBLE.
YET, NOW THAT I HELD IT IN MY HANDS, IT SEEMED ALL WRONG.
THE STAR WAS *FALLING*, WHAT SORT OF SIGIL WAS THAT?
WOULD I FALL JUST AS FAST?
AND SUNSET HERALDS NIGHT.
I SHOULD HAVE STAYED WITH THE CHALICE.
IT HAD WINGS, AT LEAS
SER ARLAN SAI
THE CUP WAS FU
OF FAITH AND
FELLOWSHIP AN
GOOD THINGS T
DRINK.
THE ELM'S ALIVE.
SEE HOW GREEN THE LEAVES ARE? SUMMER LEAVES FOR CERTAIN.
AND I'VE SEEN SHIELDS BLAZONED WITH SKULLS AND WOLVES AND RAVENS, EVEN HANGED MEN AND BLOODY HEADS.
THEY SERVED WELL ENOUGH, AND SO WILL THIS.
YOU KNOW THE OLD SHIELD RHYME? "OAK AND IRON GUARD ME WELL..."
"...OR ELSE I'M DEAD, AND DOOMED TO HELL."
I HAD NOT THOUGHT OF THAT RHYME IN YEARS.
THE OLD MAN HAD TAUGHT IT TO ME, A LONG TIME AGO.
HOW MUCH DO YOU WANT FOR THE NEW RIM AND ALL.
FROM YOU?
A COPPER.

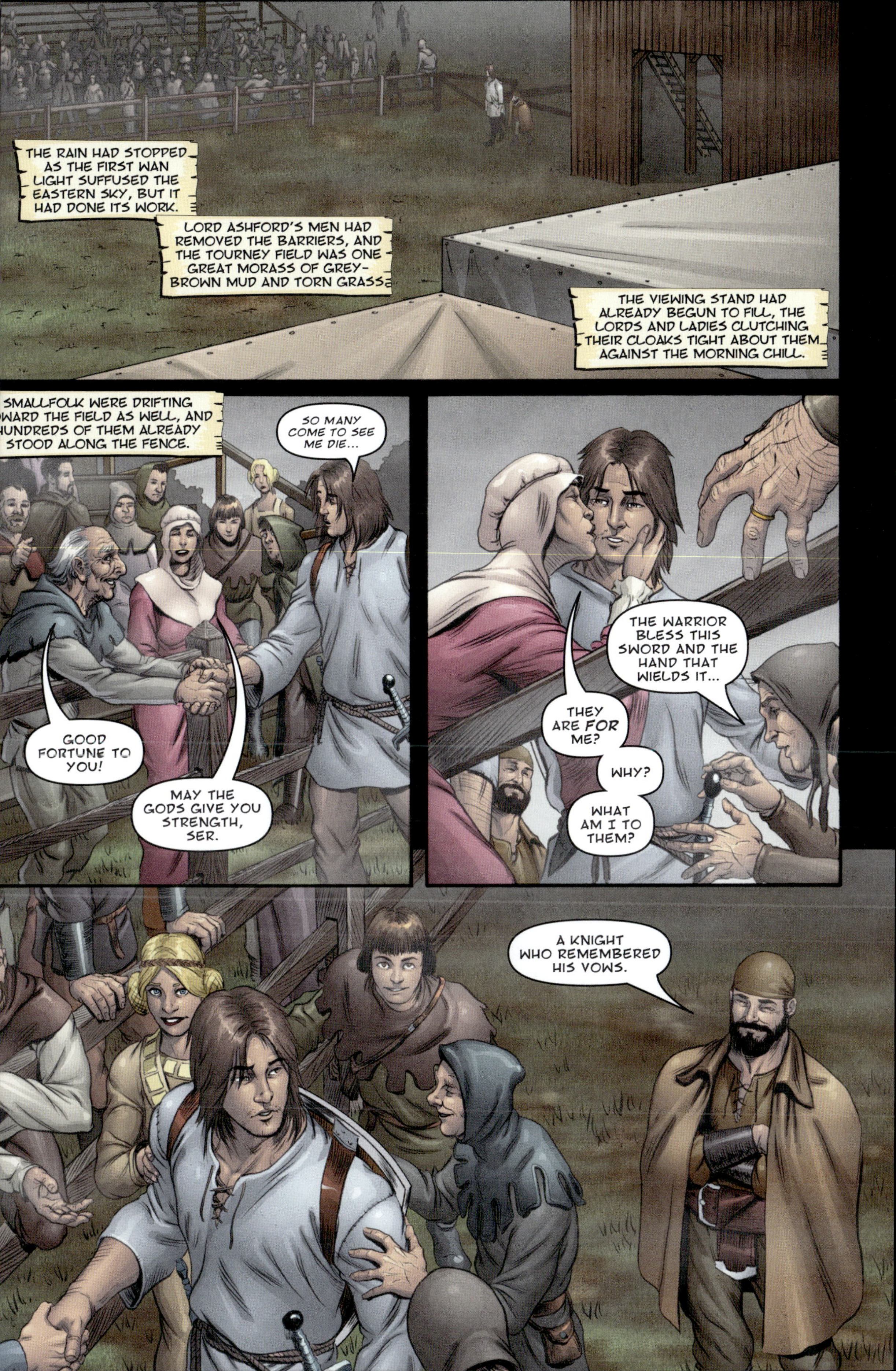

THE RAIN HAD STOPPED AS THE FIRST WAN LIGHT SUFFUSED THE EASTERN SKY, BUT IT HAD DONE ITS WORK.
LORD ASHFORD'S MEN HAD REMOVED THE BARRIERS, AND THE TOURNEY FIELD WAS ONE GREAT MORASS OF GREY-BROWN MUD AND TORN GRASS.
THE VIEWING STAND HAD ALREADY BEGUN TO FILL, THE LORDS AND LADIES CLUTCHING THEIR CLOAKS TIGHT ABOUT THEM AGAINST THE MORNING CHILL.
SMALLFOLK WERE DRIFTING TOWARD THE FIELD AS WELL, AND HUNDREDS OF THEM ALREADY STOOD ALONG THE FENCE.
SO MANY COME TO SEE ME DIE...
GOOD FORTUNE TO YOU!
MAY THE GODS GIVE YOU STRENGTH, SER.
THE WARRIOR BLESS THIS SWORD AND THE HAND THAT WIELDS IT...
THEY ARE FOR ME?
WHY?
WHAT AM I TO THEM?
A KNIGHT WHO REMEMBERED HIS VOWS.

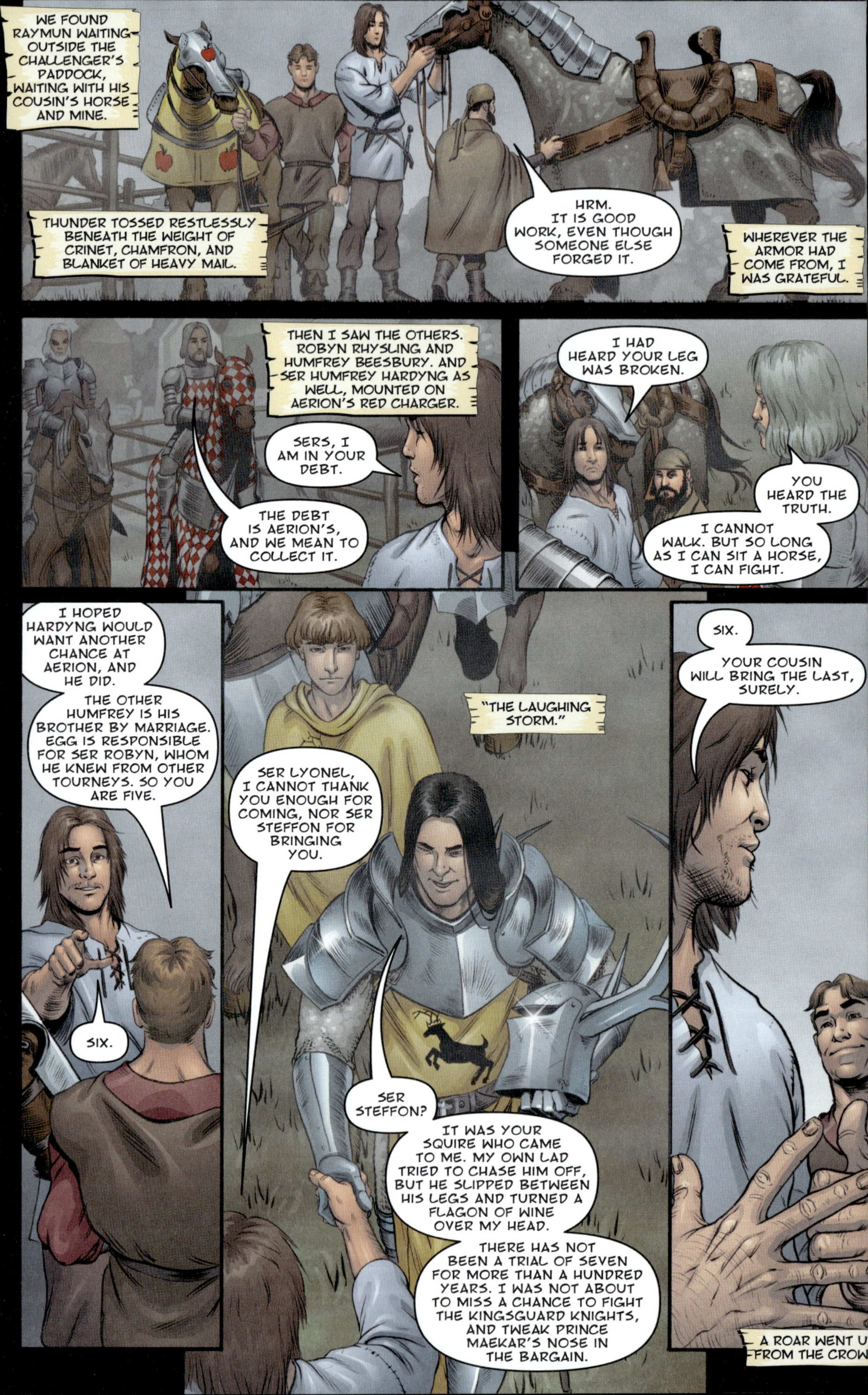
WE FOUND RAYMUN WAITING OUTSIDE THE CHALLENGER'S PADDOCK, WAITING WITH HIS COUSIN'S HORSE AND MINE.
THUNDER TOSSED RESTLESSLY BENEATH THE WEIGHT OF CRINET, CHAMFRON, AND BLANKET OF HEAVY MAIL.
HRM. IT IS GOOD WORK, EVEN THOUGH SOMEONE ELSE FORGED IT.
WHEREVER THE ARMOR HAD COME FROM, I WAS GRATEFUL.
THEN I SAW THE OTHERS. ROBYN RHYSLING AND HUMFREY BEESBURY. AND SER HUMFREY HARDYNG AS WELL, MOUNTED ON AERION'S RED CHARGER.
SERS, I AM IN YOUR DEBT.
THE DEBT IS AERION'S, AND WE MEAN TO COLLECT IT.
I HAD HEARD YOUR LEG WAS BROKEN.
YOU HEARD THE TRUTH.
I CANNOT WALK. BUT SO LONG AS I CAN SIT A HORSE, I CAN FIGHT.
I HOPED HARDYNG WOULD WANT ANOTHER CHANCE AT AERION, AND HE DID.
THE OTHER HUMFREY IS HIS BROTHER BY MARRIAGE. EGG IS RESPONSIBLE FOR SER ROBYN, WHOM HE KNEW FROM OTHER TOURNEYS. SO YOU ARE FIVE.
SIX.
"THE LAUGHING STORM."
SER LYONEL, I CANNOT THANK YOU ENOUGH FOR COMING, NOR SER STEFFON FOR BRINGING YOU.
SER STEFFON?
IT WAS YOUR SQUIRE WHO CAME TO ME. MY OWN LAD TRIED TO CHASE HIM OFF, BUT HE SLIPPED BETWEEN HIS LEGS AND TURNED A FLAGON OF WINE OVER MY HEAD.
THERE HAS NOT BEEN A TRIAL OF SEVEN FOR MORE THAN A HUNDRED YEARS. I WAS NOT ABOUT TO MISS A CHANCE TO FIGHT THE KINGSGUARD KNIGHTS, AND TWEAK PRINCE MAEKAR'S NOSE IN THE BARGAIN.
SIX.
YOUR COUSIN WILL BRING THE LAST, SURELY.

AT THE NORTH END OF THE MEADOW, A COLUMN OF KNIGHTS CAME TROTTING OUT OF THE RIVER MIST.
THE THREE KINGSGUARD CAME FIRST, LIKE GHOSTS IN THEIR GLEAMING WHITE ENAMEL ARMOR. BEHIND RODE PRINCE MAEKAR AND HIS SONS.
SIX!
THEY ARE ONLY SIX!
IT WAS TRUE. THREE BLACK KNIGHTS AND THREE WHITE.
THEY WERE SHORT A MAN AS WELL.
WHAT WOULD THAT MEAN? WOULD WE FIGHT SIX AGAINST SIX IF NEITHER FOUND A SEVENTH?
SER, IT'S TIME YOU DONNED YOUR ARMOR.
THANK YOU, SQUIRE.
IF YOU WOULD BE SO GOOD.
STEELY PATE LENT THE LAD A HAND.
HAUBERK AND GORGET, GREAVES AND GAUNTLET, COIF AND CODPIECE, THEY TURNED ME INTO STEEL, CHECKING EACH CLASP THRICE.

RAYMUN, MY MAIL, IF YOU PLEASE.
SER STEFFON, WHAT OF YOUR FRIENDS?
WE NEED ANOTHER KNIGHT TO MAKE OUR SEVEN.
YOU NEED TWO, I FEAR.
M'LORD?
TWO?
I SEE FIVE HERE. BEESBURY, RHYSLING, HARDYNG, BARATHEON, AND YOURSELF.
AND YOU. YOU'RE THE SIXTH.
I AM THE SEVENTH --
-- BUT FOR THE OTHER SIDE.
I FIGHT WITH PRINCE AERION AND THE ACCUSERS.
NO.
YES. SER DUNCAN UNDERSTANDS, I AM SURE. I HAVE A DUTY TO MY PRINCE.
YOU TOLD HIM TO RELY ON YOU.
DID I?
NO DOUBT I WAS SINCERE AT THE TIME.
BRING ME MY HORSE.
GET HIM YOURSELF!
IF YOU THINK I WANT ANY PART OF THIS, YOU'RE AS THICK AS YOU ARE VILE!
VILE?
TSK TSK TSK. GUARD YOUR TONGUE. WE'RE BOTH APPLES FROM THE SAME TREE.
AND YOU ARE MY SQUIRE. OR HAVE YOU FORGOTTEN YOUR VOWS?
NO. HAVE YOU FORGOTTEN YOURS?
YOU SWORE TO BE A KNIGHT.
I SHALL BE MORE THAN A KNIGHT BEFORE THIS DAY IS DONE.
LORD FOSSOWAY. I LIKE THE SOUND OF THAT.
I WATCHED HIM GO, MY HANDS COILED INTO FISTS, BUT MY THROAT WAS TOO RAW FOR SPEECH.
KNIGHT ME.

I WILL TAKE MY COUSIN'S PLACE. SER DUNCAN, KNIGHT ME.
RAYMUN, I... I SHOULD NOT.
YOU MUST. WITHOUT ME, YOU ARE ONLY FIVE.
THE LAD HAS THE TRUTH OF IT.
DO IT, SER DUNCAN. ANY KNIGHT CAN MAKE A KNIGHT.
A FANFARE OF TRUMPETS CUT THE MISTY MORNING AIR.
DO YOU DOUBT MY COURAGE?
NO. NOT THAT, BUT...
SER, LORD ASHFORD SUMMONS YOU!
GO TO HIM, SER DUNCAN, I'LL GIVE SQUIRE RAYMUN HIS KNIGHTHOOD.
RAYMUN OF HOUSE FOSSOWAY, IN THE NAME OF THE WARRIOR I CHARGE YOU TO BE BRAVE.
IN THE NAME OF THE FATHER I CHARGE YOU TO BE JUST.
IN THE NAME OF THE MOTHER I CHARGE YOU TO DEFEND THE YOUNG AND INNOCENT...
I LEFT THEM THERE, FEELING AS RELIVED AS I WAS GUILTY.
SER DUNCAN, IT WOULD SEEM THAT YOU HAVE ONLY FIVE CHAMPIONS.
SIX. SER LYONEL IS KNIGHTING RAYMUN FOSSOWAY.
WE WILL FIGHT YOU SIX AGAINST SEVEN.
THAT IS NOT PERMITTED, SER. IF YOU CANNOT FIND ANOTHER KNIGHT, YOU MUST BE DECLARED GUILTY OF THE CRIMES OF WHICH YOU STAND ACCUSED.
GUILTY. GUILTY OF LOOSENING A TOOTH, AND FOR THAT I MUST DIE.
M'LORD, I BEG A MOMENT.
YOU HAVE IT.

M'LORDS, DO NONE OF YOU REMEMBER SER ARLAN OF PENNYTREE?
I WAS HIS SQUIRE. WE SERVED MANY OF YOU. ATE AT YOUR TABLES AND SLEPT IN YOUR HALLS.
SER MANFRED, SER ARLAN TOOK A WOUND IN YOUR FATHER'S SERVICE.
LORD LANNISTER, SER ARLAN UNHORSED YOU ONCE IN A TOURNEY.
HE WAS A GOOD MAN, AND HE TAUGHT ME HOW TO BE A KNIGHT.
NOT ONLY SWORD AND LANCE, BUT HONOR!
A KNIGHT DEFENDS THE INNOCENT, HE SAID. THAT'S ALL I DID!
I NEED ONE MORE KNIGHT TO FIGHT BESIDE ME! ONE, THAT'S ALL!
LORD SWANN?
LORD CARON?
SER OTHO, ALL KNOW YOU FOR A GREAT CHAMPION.
JOIN US, I BEG YOU. MY CAUSE IS JUST.
THAT MAY BE, BUT IT IS YOUR CAUSE, NOT MINE.
I KNOW YOU NOT, BOY.
ARE THERE NO TRUE KNIGHTS AMONG YOU?!
HAHAHAHA
THE DRAGON IS NOT MOCKED.
I WILL TAKE SER DUNCAN'S SIDE.

A BLACK STALLION EMERGED FROM OUT OF THE RIVER MISTS, A BLACK KNIGHT ON HIS BACK.
WHO IS IT?
UNBELIEVABLE!
WOULD HE TAKE THE SIDE OF THE ACCUSED?
THE YOUNG PRINCE.
GODS BE GOOD, COULD IT BE HIM?

LORD ASHFORD MADE THE SAME MISTAKE.
PRINCE VALARR?
NO.
I DID NOT THINK TO ENTER THE LISTS AT ASHFORD, MY LORD, SO I BROUGHT NO ARMOR.
MY SON WAS GOOD ENOUGH TO LEND ME HIS.
LIFTING THE VISOR OF HIS HELM, PRINCE BAELOR SMILED ALMOST SADLY.

ISSUE SIX
COVER A
Anders Finer &
Mike S. Miller.

ISSUE SIX
COVER B

ANDERS FINER.

THE ACCUSERS WERE THROWN INTO CONFUSION.
BROTHER, HAVE YOU TAKEN LEAVE OF YOUR SENSES?
THIS MAN ATTACKED MY SON!
THIS MAN PROTECTED THE WEAK, AS EVERY TRUE KNIGHT MUST.
LET THE GODS DECIDE IF HE WAS RIGHT OR WRONG.
AS PRINCE BAELOR TROTTED TO OUR END OF THE FIELD ON HIS SON'S HUGE BLACK DESTRIER MY OTHER DEFENDERS GATHERED ROUND:
ROBYN RHYSLING AND SER LYONEL, THE HUMFREYS.
GOOD MEN ALL, BUT WERE THEY GOOD ENOUGH?
WHERE IS RAYMUN?

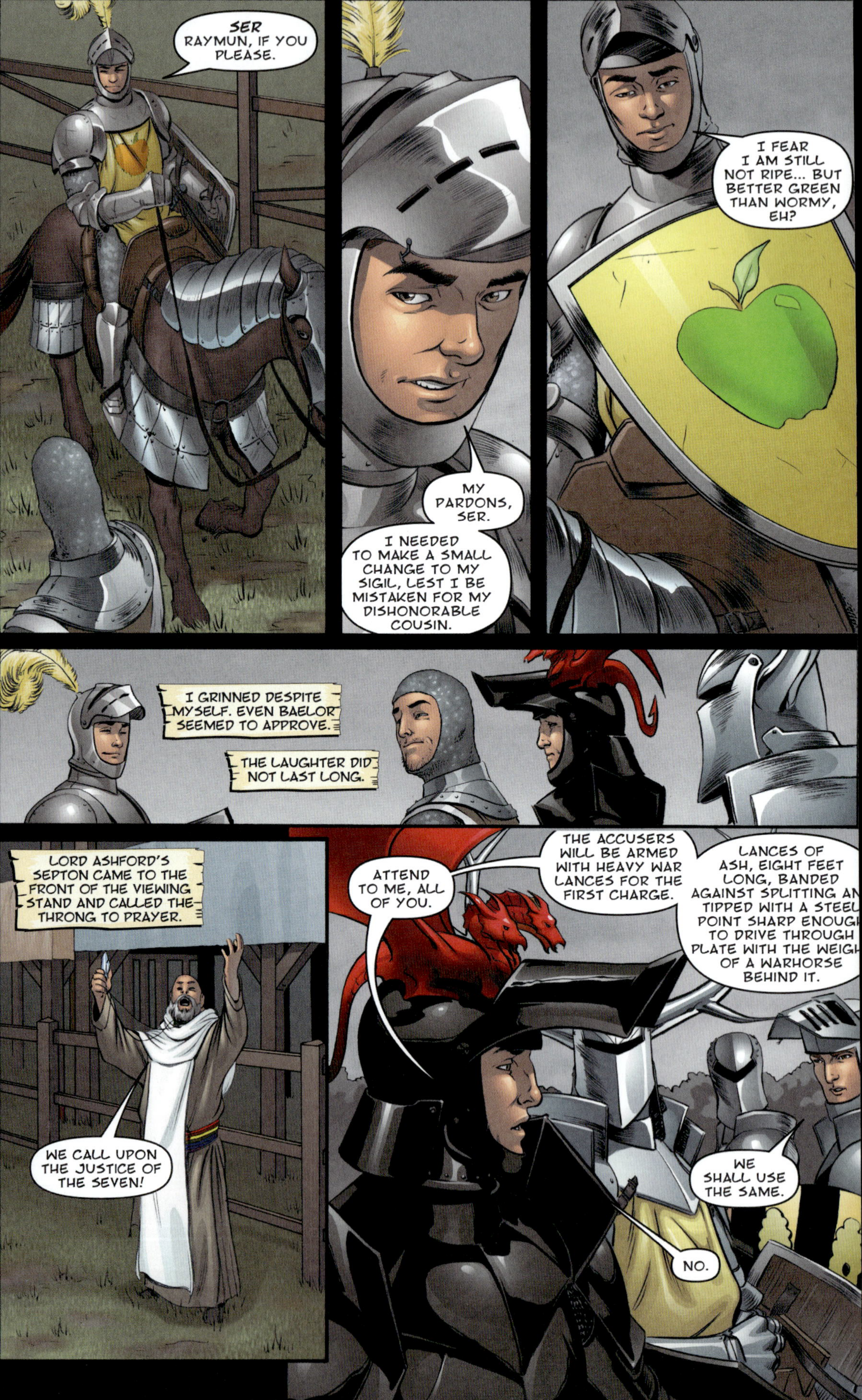
SER RAYMUN, IF YOU PLEASE.
MY PARDONS, SER.
I NEEDED TO MAKE A SMALL CHANGE TO MY SIGIL, LEST I BE MISTAKEN FOR MY DISHONORABLE COUSIN.
I FEAR I AM STILL NOT RIPE... BUT BETTER GREEN THAN WORMY, EH?
I GRINNED DESPITE MYSELF. EVEN BAELOR SEEMED TO APPROVE.
THE LAUGHTER DID NOT LAST LONG.
LORD ASHFORD'S SEPTON CAME TO THE FRONT OF THE VIEWING STAND AND CALLED THE THRONG TO PRAYER.
WE CALL UPON THE JUSTICE OF THE SEVEN!
ATTEND TO ME, ALL OF YOU.
THE ACCUSERS WILL BE ARMED WITH HEAVY WAR LANCES FOR THE FIRST CHARGE.
LANCES OF ASH, EIGHT FEET LONG, BANDED AGAINST SPLITTING AN TIPPED WITH A STEEL POINT SHARP ENOUG TO DRIVE THROUGH PLATE WITH THE WEIGH OF A WARHORSE BEHIND IT.
WE SHALL USE THE SAME.
NO.

WE WILL ARM OURSELVES WITH TOURNEY LANCES INSTEAD.
TOURNEY LANCES ARE MADE TO BREAK.
THEY ARE ALSO MADE TWELVE FEET LONG. IF OUR POINTS STRIKE HOME, THEIRS CANNOT TOUCH US.
AIM FOR HELM OR CHEST. IN A TOURNEY, IT IS A GALLANT THING TO BREAK YOUR LANCE AGAINST A FOE'S SHIELD, BUT HERE IT WILL MEAN DEATH.
IF WE CAN UNHORSE THEM AND KEEP OUR OWN SADDLES, THE ADVANTAGE IS OURS.
IF SER DUNCAN IS KILLED, IT IS CONSIDERED THAT THE GODS HAVE JUDGED HIM GUILTY AND THE CONTEST IS OVER.
IF BOTH OF HIS ACCUSERS ARE SLAIN, OR WITHDRAW THEIR ACCUSATIONS, THE SAME IS TRUE.
ELSEWISE, ALL SEVEN OF ONE SIDE OR THE OTHER MUST PERISH OR YIELD FOR THE TRIAL TO END.
PRINCE DAERON WILL NOT FIGHT.
NOT WELL, ANYWAY!
AGAINST THAT, WE HAVE THE THREE OF THE WHITE SWORDS TO CONTEND WITH.
MY BROTHER ERRED WHEN HE DEMANDED THAT THE KINGSGUARD FIGHT FOR HIS SON.
THEIR OATH FORBIDS THEM TO HARM A PRINCE OF THE BLOOD. FORTUNATELY, I AM SUCH.
KEEP THE OTHERS OFF ME LONG ENOUGH, AND I SHALL DEAL WITH THE KINGSGUARD.
MY PRINCE, IS THAT CHIVALROUS?
THE GODS WILL LET US KNOW.
...AND GRANT VICTORY TO THE MEN WHOSE CAUSE IS JUST!

A DEEP EXPECTANT SILENCE FELL ACROSS ASHFORD MEADOW.
EIGHTY YARDS AWAY, AERION'S HORSE TRUMPETED WITH IMPATIENCE AND PAWED THE MUDDY GROUND.
THUNDER WAS VERY STILL BY COMPARISON; HE WAS AN OLDER HORSE, VETERAN OF HALF A HUNDRED FIGHTS, AND HE KNEW WHAT WAS EXPECTED OF HIM.
MAY THE GODS BE WITH YOU, SER.
THE SIGHT OF MY ELM TREE AND SHOOTING STAR GAVE ME HEART.
"OAK AND IRON, GUARD ME WELL, OR ELSE I'M DEAD AND DOOMED TO HELL."
YOUR LANCE...
NO!
IT MUST BE I WHO PUTS IT IN SER DUNCAN'S HAND.
TO EITHER SIDE, MY COMPANIONS TOOK UP THEIR OWN LANCES AND SPREAD OUT IN A LONG LINE...
...BUT THE NARROW EYESLIT OF THE GREATHELM LIMITED MY VISION TO WHAT WAS DIRECTLY AHEAD.
THE VIEWING STAND WAS GONE, AND LIKEWISE THE SMALLFOLK CROWDING THE FENCE--
--THERE WAS ONLY THE MUDDY FIELD, THE PALE BLOWING MIST, AND THE PRINCELING ON HIS CHARGER WITH FLAMES ON HIS HELM AND A DRAGON ON HIS SHIELD.
I WATCHED HIS SQUIRE HAND HIM A WAR LANCE -- AERION MEANT TO PUT THAT THROUGH MY HEART...

THE HORN SOUNDED.
A STAB OF PANIC WENT THROUGH ME.
FOR A HEARTBEAT I SAT STILL AS A FLY IN AMBER.
I HAVE FORGOTTEN... I HAVE FORGOTTEN ALL, I WILL SHAME MYSELF, I WILL LOSE EVERYTHING.
THUNDER SAVED ME.
THE BIG STALLION KNEW WHAT TO DO, EVEN IF HIS RIDER DID NOT.
MY TRAINING TOOK OVER THEN.
I GAVE THE WARHORSE A LIGHT TOUCH OF SPUR, COUCHED MY LANCE, AND SWUNG MY SHIELD TO COVER MOST OF THE LEFT SIDE OF MY BODY, HOLDING IT AT AN ANGLE TO DEFLECT BLOWS AWAY...
OAK AND IRON, GUARD ME WELL...

THE NOISE OF THE CROWD WAS NO MORE THAN THE CRASH OF DISTANT WAVES.
THUNDER SLID INTO A GALLOP. MY TEETH JARRED TOGETHER WITH THE VIOLENCE OF THE PACE.

I PRESSED MY HEELS DOWN, TIGHTENING MY LEGS WITH ALL MY STRENGTH AND LETTING MY BODY BECOME PART OF THE MOTION OF THE HORSE BENEATH.
THE AIR INSIDE MY HELM WAS ALREADY SO HOT I COULD SCARCELY BREATH...

IN A TOURNEY JOUST, MY FOE WOULD BE TO MY LEFT ACROSS THE TILTING BARRIER. THE ANGLE MADE IT MORE LIKELY THAT THE WOOD WOULD BE SPLIT ON IMPACT.
BUT THIS WAS A DEADLIER GAME. WITH NO BARRIERS DIVIDING US, THE DESTRIERS CHARGED STRAIGHT AT ONE ANOTHER.
I GLIMPSED BAELOR'S HUGE BLACK POUNDING AHEAD THROUGH THE CORNER OF MY EYE SLIT.
I SENSED MORE THAN SAW THE OTHERS.
THEY DID NOT MATTER.
ONLY AERION MATTERED. ONLY HIM.
I WATCHED THE DRAGON COME, THE BLACK LANCE STILL ANGLED UPWARD.
A KNIGHT WHO HOLDS HIS LANCE HIGH AND BRINGS IT ON LINE AT THE LAST MOMENT ALWAYS RISKS LOWERING IT TOO FAR, THE OLD MAN HAD TOLD ME.
MY LANCE IS PART OF MY ARM...
IT'S MY FINGER, A WOODEN FINGER...
ALL I NEED DO IS TOUCH HIM WITH MY LONG WOODEN FINGER...
I TRIED NOT TO SEE THE SHARP IRON POINT AT THE END OF AERION'S BLACK LANCE, GROWING LARGER EVERY STRIDE.
"THE DRAGON, LOOK AT THE DRAGON," I THOUGHT, THEN REMEMBERED SUDDENLY, "NO! LOOK ONLY WHERE YOU MEAN TO STRIKE!"
BUT I WAS TOO LATE.
CRACK

UP!
UP, THUNDER!
AND SOMEHOW THE OLD WARHORSE FOUND HIS FEET AGAIN.
I COULD FEEL A SHARP PAIN UNDER MY RIB.
AERION HAD DRIVEN HIS LANCE THROUGH OAK, WOOL, AND STEEL; THREE FEET OF SPLINTERED ASH AND SHARP IRON STUCK FROM MY SIDE.

AAARRRGH!
THE WORLD SWAM AND I ALMOST FELL.
DIMLY, THROUGH THE PAIN, I COULD HEAR VOICES CALLING MY NAME.
MY BEAUTIFUL SHIELD WAS USELESS NOW.
I TOSSED IT ASIDE, ELM TREE, SHOOTING STAR, BROKEN LANCE AND ALL.
I DREW MY SWORD, BUT I HURT SO MUCH I DID NOT THINK I COULD SWING IT.
TURNING THUNDER IN A TIGHT CIRCLE, I TRIED TO GET A SENSE OF WHAT WAS HAPPENING ELSEWHERE.

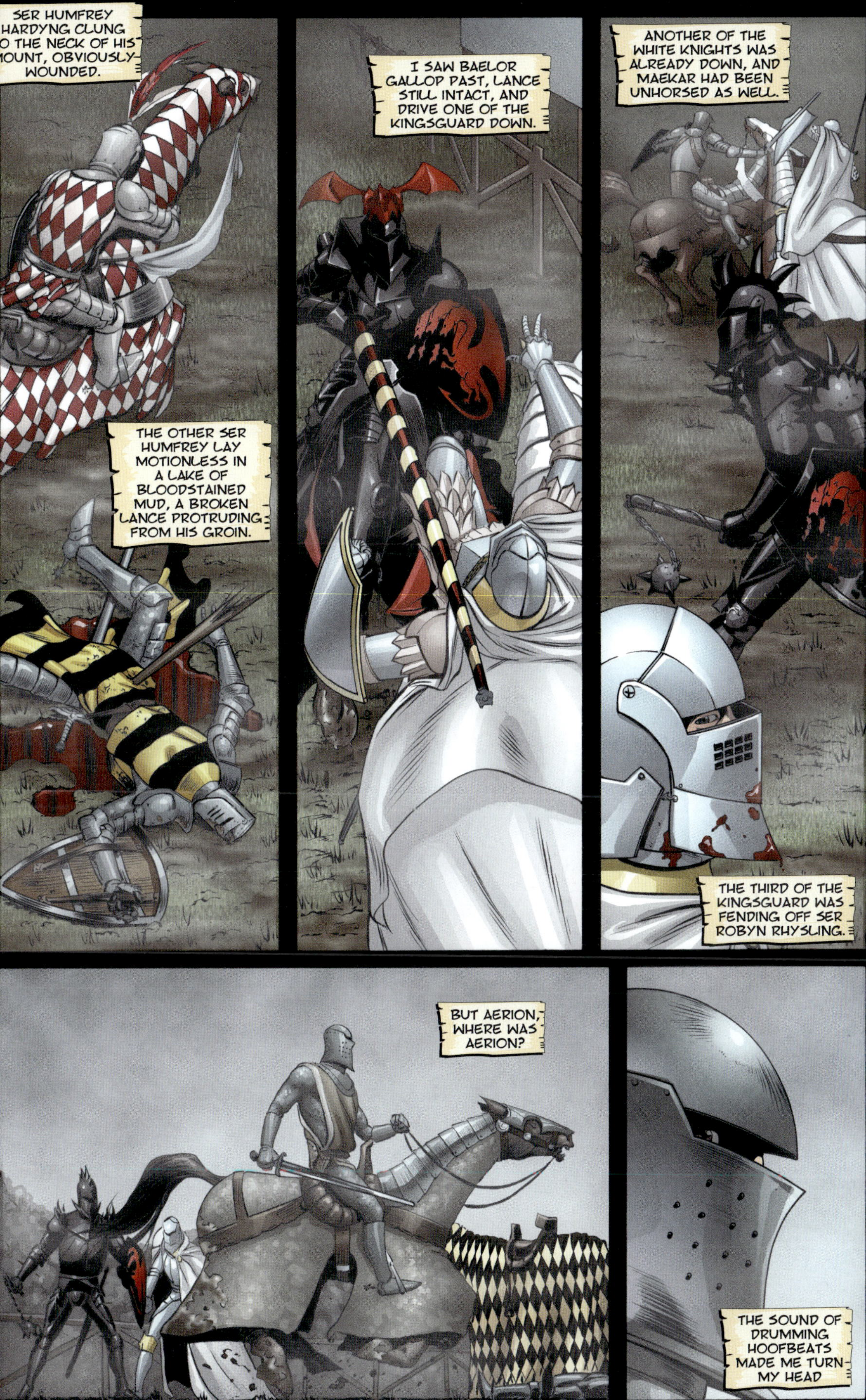
SER HUMFREY HARDYNG CLUNG TO THE NECK OF HIS MOUNT, OBVIOUSLY WOUNDED.
THE OTHER SER HUMFREY LAY MOTIONLESS IN A LAKE OF BLOODSTAINED MUD, A BROKEN LANCE PROTRUDING FROM HIS GROIN.
I SAW BAELOR GALLOP PAST, LANCE STILL INTACT, AND DRIVE ONE OF THE KINGSGUARD DOWN.
ANOTHER OF THE WHITE KNIGHTS WAS ALREADY DOWN, AND MAEKAR HAD BEEN UNHORSED AS WELL.
THE THIRD OF THE KINGSGUARD WAS FENDING OFF SER ROBYN RHYSLING.
BUT AERION, WHERE WAS AERION?
THE SOUND OF DRUMMING HOOFBEATS MADE ME TURN MY HEAD

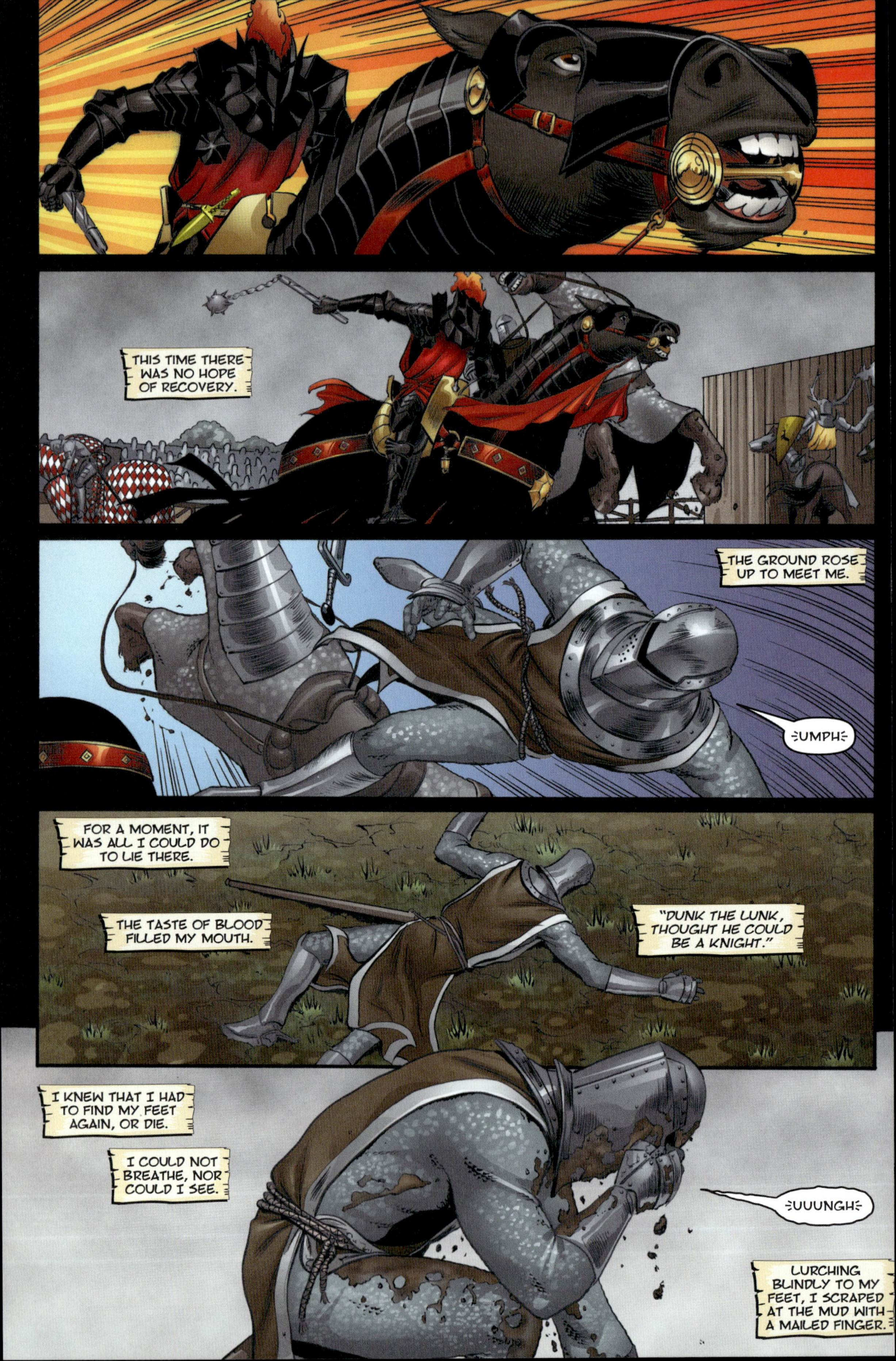
THIS TIME THERE WAS NO HOPE OF RECOVERY.
THE GROUND ROSE UP TO MEET ME.
UMPH
FOR A MOMENT, IT WAS ALL I COULD DO TO LIE THERE.
THE TASTE OF BLOOD FILLED MY MOUTH.
"DUNK THE LUNK, THOUGHT HE COULD BE A KNIGHT."
I KNEW THAT I HAD TO FIND MY FEET AGAIN, OR DIE.
I COULD NOT BREATHE, NOR COULD I SEE.
UUUNGH
LURCHING BLINDLY TO MY FEET, I SCRAPED AT THE MUD WITH A MAILED FINGER.

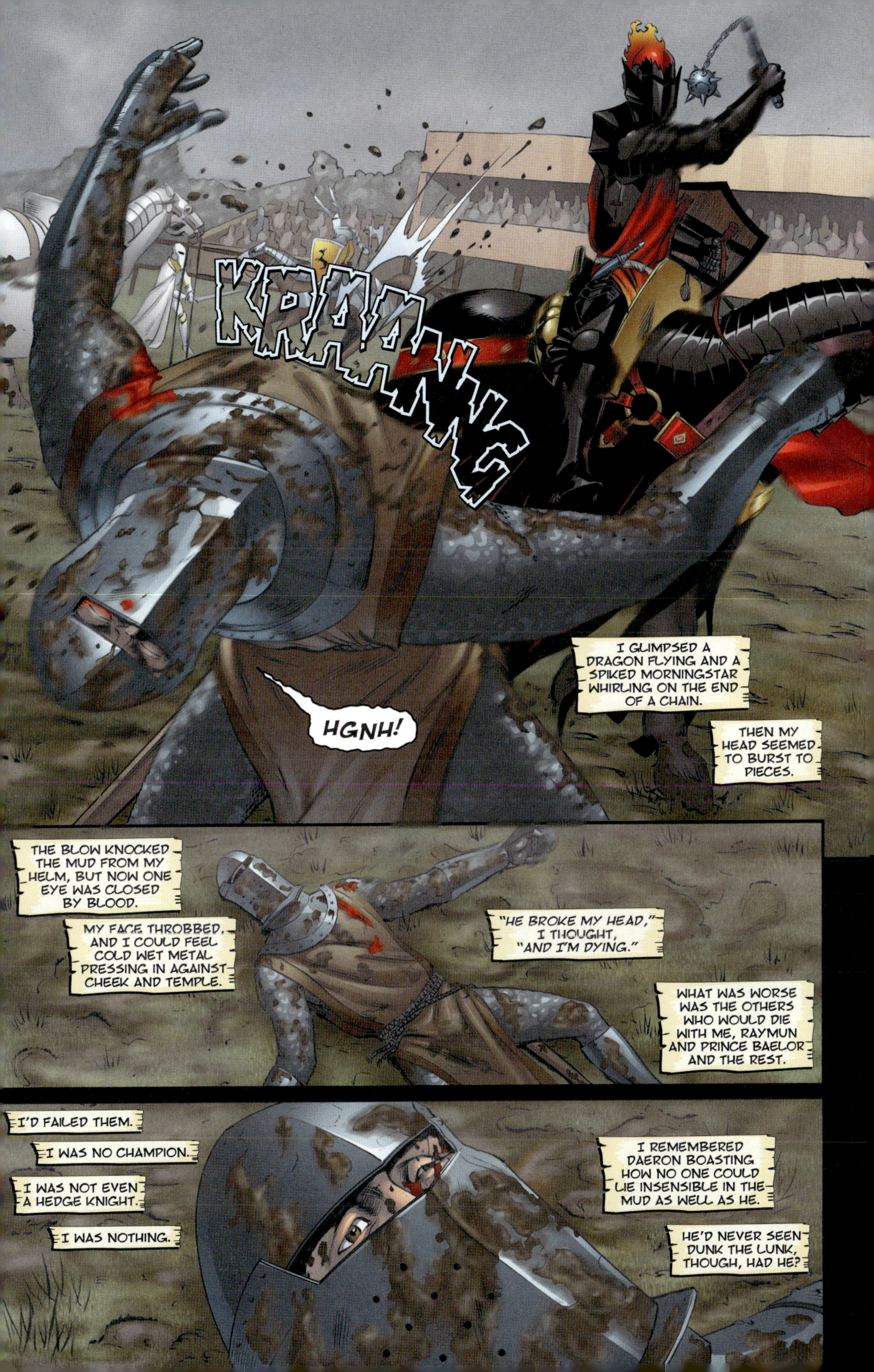
KRAANNG
I GLIMPSED A DRAGON FLYING AND A SPIKED MORNINGSTAR WHIRLING ON THE END OF A CHAIN.
HGNH!
THEN MY HEAD SEEMED TO BURST TO PIECES.
THE BLOW KNOCKED THE MUD FROM MY HELM, BUT NOW ONE EYE WAS CLOSED BY BLOOD.
MY FACE THROBBED, AND I COULD FEEL COLD WET METAL PRESSING IN AGAINST CHEEK AND TEMPLE.
"HE BROKE MY HEAD," I THOUGHT, "AND I'M DYING."
WHAT WAS WORSE WAS THE OTHERS WHO WOULD DIE WITH ME, RAYMUN AND PRINCE BAELOR AND THE REST.
I'D FAILED THEM.
I WAS NO CHAMPION.
I WAS NOT EVEN A HEDGE KNIGHT.
I WAS NOTHING.
I REMEMBERED DAERON BOASTING HOW NO ONE COULD LIE INSENSIBLE IN THE MUD AS WELL AS HE.
HE'D NEVER SEEN DUNK THE LUNK, THOUGH, HAD HE?

ARE YOU NOT DEAD YET, HEDGE KNIGHT?
THE DRAGON APPEARED ABOVE ME.
CRY FOR QUARTER AND ADMIT YOUR GUILT, AND PERHAPS I'LL ONLY CLAIM A HAND AND A FOOT.
OH, AND THOSE TEETH, BUT WHAT ARE A FEW TEETH? A MAN LIKE YOU CAN LIVE ON PEASE PORRIDGE.
NO?
EAT THIS, THEN.

WHERE I FOUND THE STRENGTH I DID NOT KNOW, BUT I FOUND IT.
WHUMP
KRRUNKK
SNAP

THE SHIELD WAS THICKER THAN MINE HAD BEEN.
SOLID OAK, BANDED WITH IRON.
WHAM
I BROUGHT IT DOWN ON TOP OF THE PRINCELING'S HELM, AGAIN AND AGAIN AND AGAIN...
WHAM
THE PRINCE RAN OUT OF FLAMES LONG BEFORE I RAN OUT OF BLOWS.
WHAM
HE COULD VANQUISH SER DUNCAN THE TALL...
...BUT NOT DUNK OF FLEA BOTTOM.

THE OLD MAN HAD TAUGHT ME JOUSTING AND SWORDPLAY, BUT THIS SORT OF FIGHTING I LEARNED EARLIER...
...IN SHADOWY WYNDS AND CROOKED ALLEYS BEHIND THE CITY'S WINESINKS.
AERION'S EYES WERE PURPLE AND FULL OF TERROR, AND I HAD A SUDDEN URGE TO GRAB ONE AND POP IT LIKE A GRAPE.
BUT THAT WOULD NOT BE KNIGHTLY.
YIELD!
I YIELD.

FOR A MOMENT I COULD NOT CREDIT WHAT MY EARS HAD HEARD.
WAS IT DONE, THEN?
AT ONCE I WAS DROWNED IN SIGHTS AND SOUNDS; GRUNTS AND CURSES, THE SHOUTS OF THE CROWD, A STALLION SCREAMING. EVERYWHERE STEEL RANG ON STEEL.
RAYMUN AND HIS COUSIN WERE SLASHING AT EACH OTHER; THEIR SHIELDS WERE SPLINTERED RUINS, THE GREEN APPLE AND THE RED BOTH HACKED TO TINDER.
ONE OF THE KINGSGUARD KNIGHTS WAS CARRYING A WOUNDED BROTHER FROM THE FIELD AND THE THIRD WAS DOWN.
THE LAUGHING STORM HAD JOINED PRINCE BAELOR AGAINST PRINCE MAEKAR.
MACE, BATTLE AX, AND LONGSWORD CLASHED AND CLANGED, RINGING AGAINST HELM AND SHIELD.
MAEKAR WAS TAKIN THREE BLOWS FOR EVERY ONE HE LANDED, AND I COUL SEE THAT IT WOULD BE OVER SOON.
I MUST MAKE AN END TO THIS BEFORE MORE OF US ARE KILLED.

THUMP
BY THE TIME WE REACHED THE VIEWING STAND WHERE LORD ASHFORD SAT, THE BRIGHT PRINCE WAS AS BROWN AS A PRIVY.
TELL HIM!
I WITHDRAW MY ACCUSATION.

AFTERWARD I COULD NOT HAVE SAID WHETHER I WALKED FROM THE FIELD UNDER MY OWN POWER OR HAD REQUIRED HELP.
I HURT EVERYWHERE, AND SOME PLACES WORSE THAN OTHERS.
EGG HELPED ME REMOVE MY GREAVES AND GORGET, AND RAYMUN AS WELL, AND EVEN STEELY PATE.
I WAS TOO DAZED TO TELL THEM APART. THEY WERE FINGERS AND THUMBS AND VOICES.
LOOK AT WHAT HE'S DONE TO ME ARMOR!
PATE WAS THE ONE COMPLAINING, I KNEW.
ALL DINTED AND BANGED AND SCRATCHED!
AYE, I ASK YOU, WHY DO I BOTHER?
I'LL HAVE TO CUT THE MAIL OFF HIM, I FEAR.
RAYMUN, THE OTHERS. HOW DID THEY FARE?
HAS ANYONE DIED?
BEESBURY.
SLAIN BY DONNEL OF DUSKENDALE IN THE FIRST CHARGE.
SER HUMFREY IS GRAVELY WOUNDED AS WELL. THE REST ARE BRUISED AND BLOODY, NO MORE.
SAVE FOR YOU.
AND THE ACCUSERS?

SER WILLEM WYLDE OF THE KINGSGUARD WAS CARRIED FROM THE FIELD INSENSATE, AND I THINK I CRACKED A FEW OF MY COUSIN'S RIBS.
AT LEAST, I HOPE SO.
AND PRINCE DAERON?
DID HE SURVIVE?
ONCE SER ROBYN UNHORSED HIM, HE LAY WHERE HE FELL. HE MAY HAVE A BROKEN FOOT.
HIS OWN HORSE TROD ON HIM WHILE RUNNING LOOSE ON THE FIELD.
DAZED AND CONFUSED AS I WAS, I FELT A HUGE SENSE OF RELIEF.
HIS DREAM WAS WRONG, THEN.
THE DEAD DRAGON.
UNLESS AERION DIED. HE DIDN'T THOUGH, DID HE?
NO. YOU SPARED HIM.
DON'T YOU REMEMBER?
I SUPPOSE.
ALREADY THE MEMORIES OF THE FIGHT WERE BECOMING CONFUSED AND VAGUE.
ONE MOMENT I FEEL DRUNK. THE NEXT IT HURTS SO BAD I KNOW I'M DYING.
LIE DOWN, SER DUNCAN.
GODS BE GOOD, THE LANCE POINT DROVE THE RINGS DEEP INTO HIS FLESH.

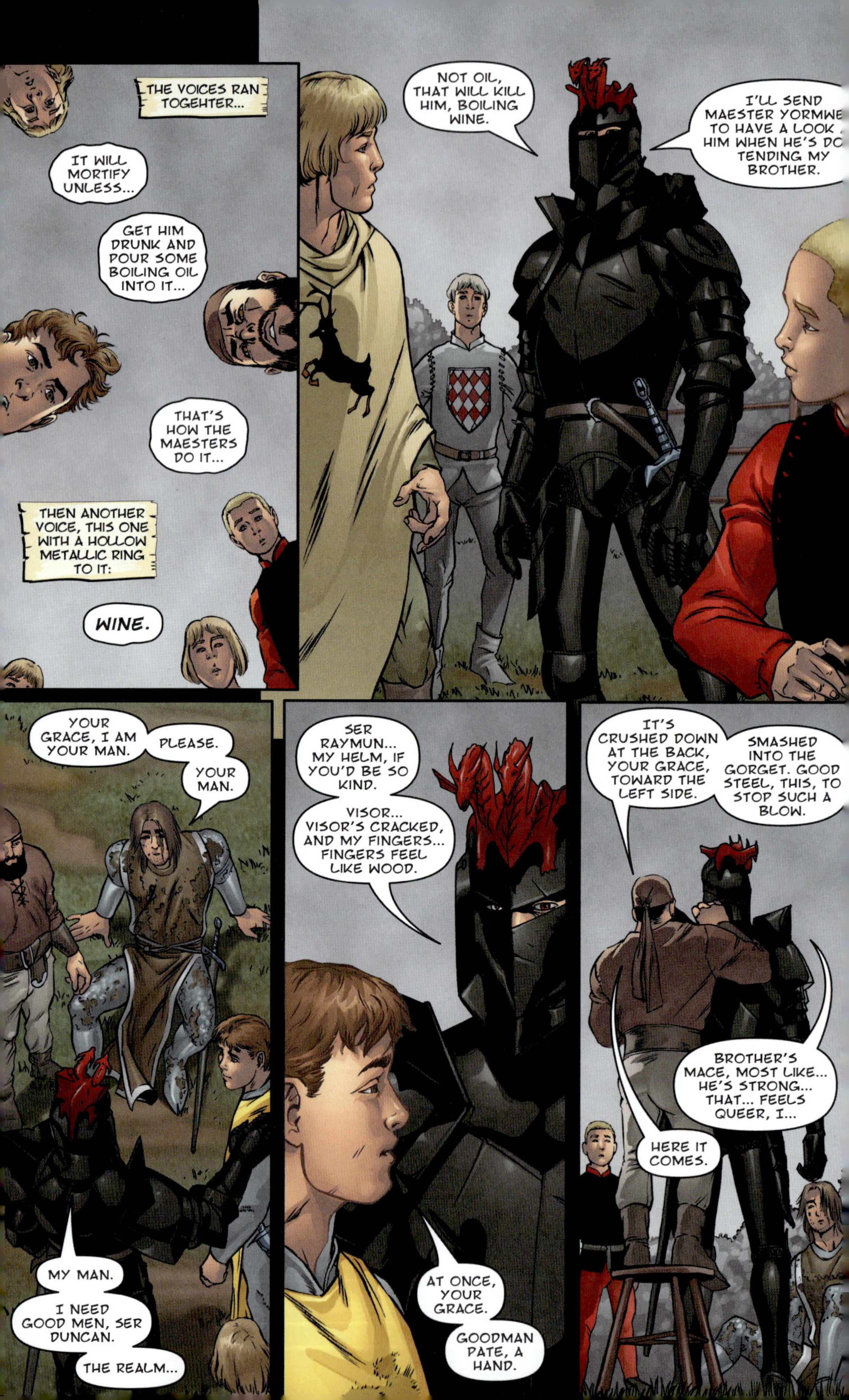
THE VOICES RAN TOGEHTER...
IT WILL MORTIFY UNLESS...
GET HIM DRUNK AND POUR SOME BOILING OIL INTO IT...
THAT'S HOW THE MAESTERS DO IT...
THEN ANOTHER VOICE, THIS ONE WITH A HOLLOW METALLIC RING TO IT:
WINE.
NOT OIL, THAT WILL KILL HIM, BOILING WINE.
I'LL SEND MAESTER YORMWE TO HAVE A LOOK HIM WHEN HE'S DO TENDING MY BROTHER.
YOUR GRACE, I AM YOUR MAN.
PLEASE.
YOUR MAN.
MY MAN.
I NEED GOOD MEN, SER DUNCAN.
THE REALM...
SER RAYMUN... MY HELM, IF YOU'D BE SO KIND.
VISOR... VISOR'S CRACKED, AND MY FINGERS... FINGERS FEEL LIKE WOOD.
AT ONCE, YOUR GRACE.
GOODMAN PATE, A HAND.
IT'S CRUSHED DOWN AT THE BACK, YOUR GRACE, TOWARD THE LEFT SIDE.
SMASHED INTO THE GORGET. GOOD STEEL, THIS, TO STOP SUCH A BLOW.
BROTHER'S MACE, MOST LIKE... HE'S STRONG... THAT... FEELS QUEER, I...
HERE IT COMES.

GODS BE GOOD.
OH GODS. OH GODS, OH GODS! OH GODS PRESERVE...
SAW SOMETHING ED AND WET FALL UT OF THE HELM.
SOMEONE WAS SCREAMING, HIGH AND TERRIBLE.
A QUEER, TROUBLED LOOK PASSED ACROSS BAELOR'S FACE, LIKE A CLOUD PASSING BEFORE THE SUN.
AGAINST THE BLEAK GREY SKY SWAYED A TALL TALL PRINCE IN BLACK ARMOR WITH ONLY HALF A SKULL.
I CAUGHT HIM.
"UP," THEY SAY I SAID, JUST AS I HAD WITH THUNDER IN THE MELEE, "UP, UP."
BUT I NEVER REMEMBERED THAT AFTERWARD, AND THE PRINCE DID NOT RISE.

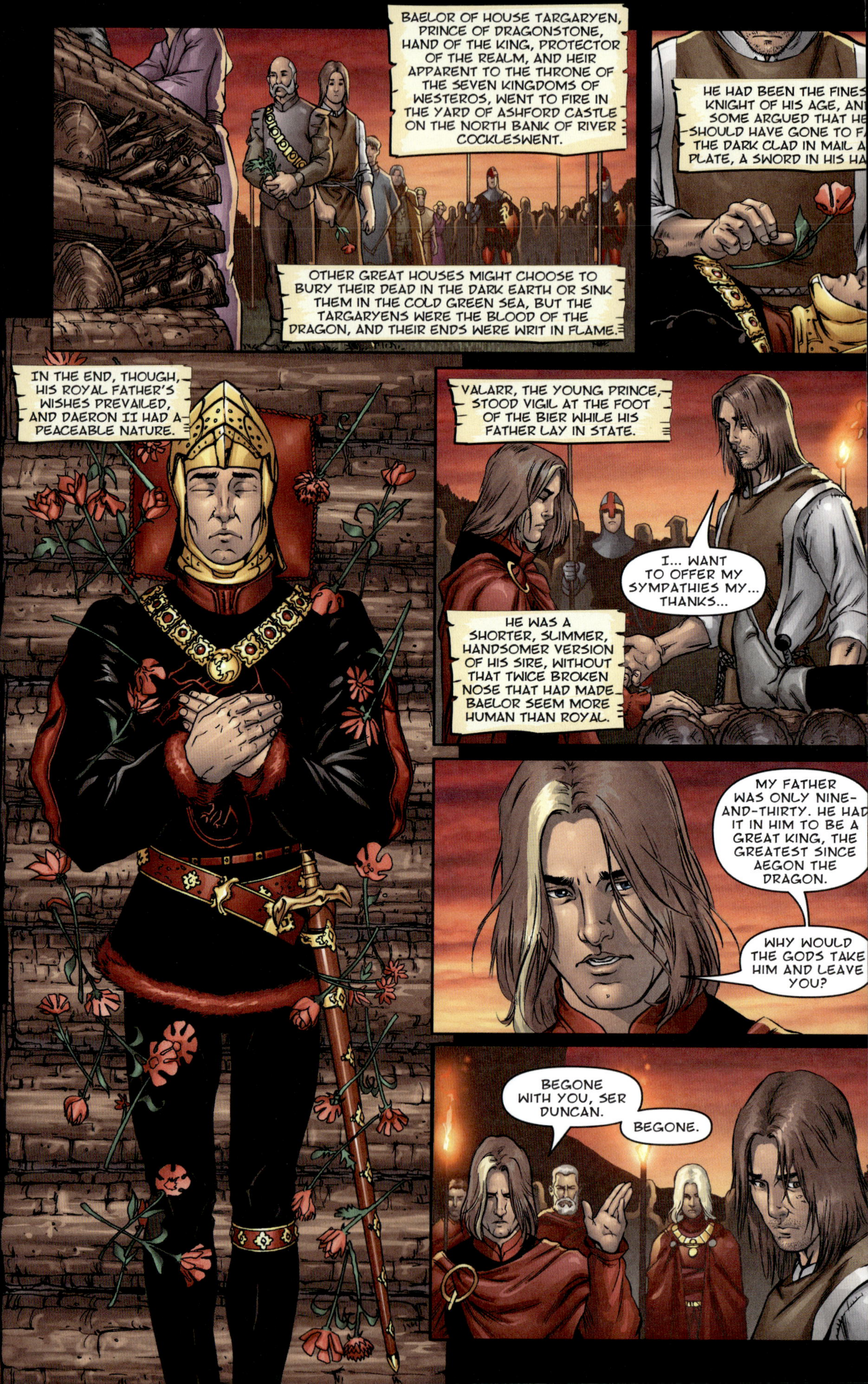
BAELOR OF HOUSE TARGARYEN, PRINCE OF DRAGONSTONE, HAND OF THE KING, PROTECTOR OF THE REALM, AND HEIR APPARENT TO THE THRONE OF THE SEVEN KINGDOMS OF WESTEROS, WENT TO FIRE IN THE YARD OF ASHFORD CASTLE ON THE NORTH BANK OF RIVER COCKLESWENT.
OTHER GREAT HOUSES MIGHT CHOOSE TO BURY THEIR DEAD IN THE DARK EARTH OR SINK THEM IN THE COLD GREEN SEA, BUT THE TARGARYENS WERE THE BLOOD OF THE DRAGON, AND THEIR ENDS WERE WRIT IN FLAME.
HE HAD BEEN THE FINES KNIGHT OF HIS AGE, AN SOME ARGUED THAT HE SHOULD HAVE GONE TO F THE DARK CLAD IN MAIL A PLATE, A SWORD IN HIS HA
IN THE END, THOUGH, HIS ROYAL FATHER'S WISHES PREVAILED, AND DAERON II HAD A PEACEABLE NATURE.
VALARR, THE YOUNG PRINCE, STOOD VIGIL AT THE FOOT OF THE BIER WHILE HIS FATHER LAY IN STATE.
I... WANT TO OFFER MY SYMPATHIES MY... THANKS...
HE WAS A SHORTER, SLIMMER, HANDSOMER VERSION OF HIS SIRE, WITHOUT THAT TWICE BROKEN NOSE THAT HAD MADE BAELOR SEEM MORE HUMAN THAN ROYAL.
MY FATHER WAS ONLY NINE-AND-THIRTY. HE HAD IT IN HIM TO BE A GREAT KING, THE GREATEST SINCE AEGON THE DRAGON.
WHY WOULD THE GODS TAKE HIM AND LEAVE YOU?
BEGONE WITH YOU, SER DUNCAN.
BEGONE.

I HAD NO ANSWER FOR VALARR.
NOR FOR THE QUESTIONS I ASKED MYSELF.
THE MAESTERS AND THE BOILING WINE HAD DONE THEIR WORK, AND MY WOUND WAS HEALING CLEANLY, THOUGH THERE WOULD BE A DEEP PUCKERED SCAR BETWEEN MY LEFT ARM AND MY NIPPLE.
I COULD NOT SEE THE WOUND WITHOUT THINKING OF BAELOR.
HE SAVED ME ONCE WITH HIS SWORD, AND ONCE WITH HIS WORD, EVEN THOUGH HE WAS A DEAD MAN AS HE STOOD THERE.
THE WORLD MADE NO SENSE WHEN A GREAT PRINCE DIED SO A HEDGE KNIGHT MIGHT LIVE.

SOON AFTER, WHEN MAEKAR AND FOUR GUARDSMEN IN THE ROYAL LIVERY APPEARED IN MY CAMP LATE ONE DAY, I WAS SURE THEY HAD COME TO KILL ME AFTER ALL.
INSTEAD:
A WORD WITH YOU, SER DUNCAN.
I HAVE SENT AERION TO LYS. A FEW YEARS IN THE FREE CITIES MAY CHANGE HIM FOR THE BETTER.
I DID NOT KNOW WHAT TO SAY, ALTHOUGH I WAS PLEASED THAT AERION WAS GONE FROM THE SEVEN KINGDOMS.
SOME MEN WILL SAY I MEANT TO KILL MY BROTHER. THE GODS KNOW IT IS A LIE, BUT I WILL HEAR THE WHISPERS UNTIL THE DAY I DIE.
AND IT WAS MY MACE THAT DEALT THE FATAL BLOW, I HAVE NO DOUBT. STRANGE TO SAY, I DO NOT RECALL THE BLOW THAT BROKE HIS SKULL.
IS THAT A MERCY OR A CURSE? SOME OF BOTH, I THINK.
I COULD NOT SAY, YOUR GRACE.
YOU SWUNG THE MACE, M'LORD, BUT IT WAS FOR ME PRINCE BAELOR DIED. SO I KILLED HIM TOO, AS MUCH AS YOU.
YES.
YOU'LL HEAR THEM WHISPER AS WELL. WHEN THE KING DIES, VALARR WILL CLIMB THE IRON THRONE IN PLACE OF HIS FATHER.
EACH TIME A BATTLE IS LOST OR A CROP FAILS, THE FOOLS WILL SAY, "BAELOR WOULD NEVER LET THIS HAPPEN, BUT THE HEDGE KNIGHT KILLED HIM."
SOMETIMES I SIT UNDER THAT TREE THERE AND ASK HOW COULD MY FOOT BE WORTH A PRINCE'S LIFE?
AND WHAT ANSWER DOES YOUR TREE GIVE YOU?
NONE. BUT THE OLD MAN, SER ARLAN, EVERY DAY AT EVENFALL HE'D SAY, "I WONDER WHAT THE MORROW WILL BRING."
WELL, MIGHTEN IT BE THAT SOME MORROW WILL COME WHEN I'LL HAVE NEED OF THAT FOOT? WHEN THE REALM WILL NEED THAT FOOT, EVEN MORE THAN A PRINCE'S LIFE?
IT'S NOT BLOODY LIKELY.
THE REALM HAS AS MANY HEDGE KNIGHTS AS HEDGES, AND ALL OF THEM HAVE FEET.
IF YOUR GRACE HAS A BETTER ANSWER, I'D LIKE TO HEAR IT.
I'D ASK THE HIGH SEPTON, BUT THE LAST TIME I WENT TO HIM HE TOLD ME THAT NO MAN CAN TRULY UNDERSTAND THE WORKINGS OF THE GODS.
PERHAPS HE SHOULD TRY SLEEPING UNDER A TREE.
MY YOUNGEST SON SEEMS TO HAVE GROWN FOND OF YOU, SER.
IT IS TIME HE WAS A SQUIRE, BUT HE TELLS ME HE WILL SERVE NO KNIGHT BUT YOU.
HE IS AN UNRULY BOY, AS YOU WILL HAVE NOTICED. WILL YOU HAVE HIM?
ME?

EGG... AEGON, I MEAN... HE IS A GOOD LAD, BUT, YOUR GRACE, I KNOW YOU HONOR ME, BUT... I AM ONLY A HEDGE KNIGHT.
THAT CAN BE CHANGED. THERE IS A PLACE FOR YOU IN MY HOUSEHOLD, IF YOU WISH. YOU'LL SWEAR YOUR SWORD TO ME, AND AEGON WILL SQUIRE FOR YOU. WHILE YOU TRAIN HIM, MY MASTER-AT-ARMS WILL FINISH YOUR TRAINING.
YOU STILL HAVE MUCH TO LEARN.
I KNOW, M'LORD.
I LOOKED ABOUT ME. AT THE GREEN GRASS AND TALL REEDS, THE TALL ELM. ANOTHER DRAGONFLY WAS MOVING ACROSS THE WATER. OR PERHAPS IT WAS THE SAME ONE.
WHAT WAS IT TO BE? DRAGONFLIES OR DRAGONS?
JUST BEFORE PRINCE BAELOR DIED, I SWORE TO BE HIS MAN.
PRESUMPTUOUS OF YOU. WHAT DID HE SAY?
THAT THE REALM NEEDED GOOD MEN.
THAT'S TRUE ENOUGH. WHAT OF IT?
I WILL TAKE YOUR SON AS SQUIRE, YOUR GRACE, BUT NOT AT SUMMERHALL. NOT FOR A YEAR OR TWO.
I'LL HAVE HIM ONLY IF I CAN TAKE HIM ON THE ROAD WITH ME.
HE'LL RIDE MY STEED, WEAR MY OLD CLOAK, AND HE'LL KEEP MY SWORD SHARP AND MY MAIL SCOURED. WE'LL SLEEP IN INNS AND STABLES, AND NOW AND AGAIN IN THE HALLS OF SOME LANDED KNIGHT OR LESSER LORDLING, AND MAYBE UNDER THE TREES WHEN WE MUST.
DID THE TRIAL ADDLE YOUR WITS, MAN?
AEGON IS A PRINCE OF THE REALM. THE BLOOD OF DRAGONS!
PRINCES ARE NOT MADE FOR SLEEPING IN DITCHES AND EATING HARD SALT BEEF.
DAERON NEVER SLEPT IN A DITCH, I'LL WAGER, AND ALL THE BEEF AERION EVER ATE WAS THICK AND RARE AND BLOODY, LIKE AS NOT.
I HEARD HIM RIDING OFF WITH HIS MEN.
WHEN THEY WERE GONE, THERE WAS NO SOUND BUT THE FAINT THRUM OF THE DRAGONFLY'S WINGS AS IT SKIMMED ACROSS THE WATER.

MY LORD FATHER SAYS I AM TO SERVE YOU.
"SERVE YOU, SER."
YOU CAN START BY SADDLING THE HORSES.
CHESTNUT IS YOURS, TREAT HER KINDLY. I DON'T WANT TO FIND YOU ON THUNDER UNLESS I PUT YOU THERE.
WHERE ARE WE GOING, SER?
I HAVE NEVER BEEN OVER THE RED MOUNTAINS.
WOULD YOU LIKE TO HAVE A LOOK AT DORNE?
I HEAR THEY HAVE GOOD PUPPET SHOWS.

PREVIEW OF FORTHCOMING

The Hedge Knight
The Sworn Sword

Battle on Redgrass Field

& VARIANT COVERS AND SKETCHES BY
MIKE S. MILLER FROM THE HEDGE KNIGHT

JET CITY COMICS

The Hedge Knight

The Sworn Sword

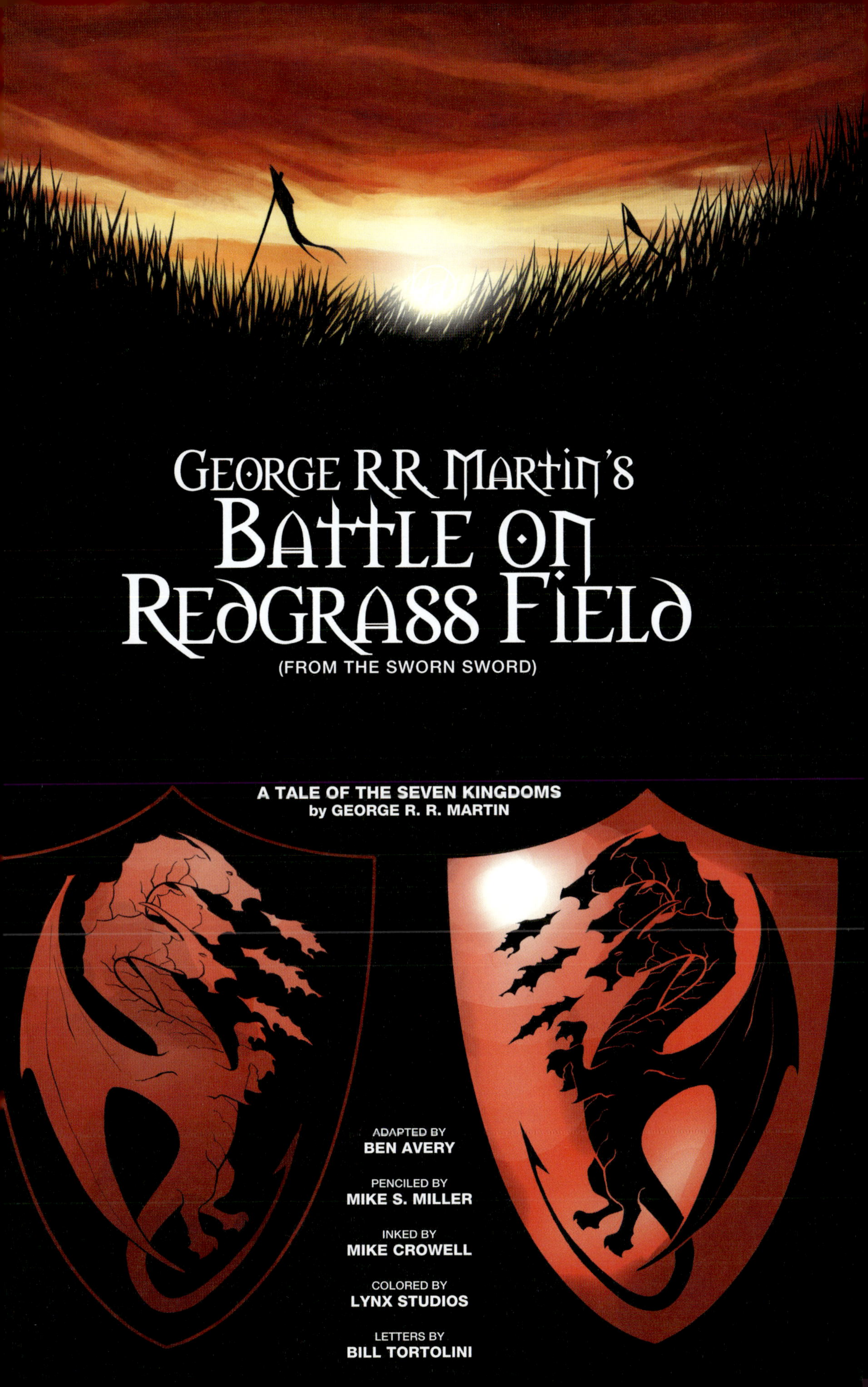
GEORGE RR MARTIN'S
BATTLE ON REDGRASS FIELD
(FROM THE SWORN SWORD)
A TALE OF THE SEVEN KINGDOMS
by GEORGE R. R. MARTIN
ADAPTED BY
BEN AVERY
PENCILED BY
MIKE S. MILLER
INKED BY
MIKE CROWELL
COLORED BY
LYNX STUDIOS
LETTERS BY
BILL TORTOLINI

MANY GOOD MEN FELL ON THAT DAY, ON BOTH SIDES. THE GRASS WAS NOT RED BEFORE THE BATTLE. DID YOUR SER ARLAN TELL YOU THAT?
SER ARLAN NEVER LIKED TO SPEAK ABOUT THE BATTLE. HIS SQUIRE DIED THERE. ROGER OF PENNYTREE WAS HIS NAME, SER ARLAN'S SISTER'S SON.
I FELT VAGUELY GUILTY. I STOLE ROGER'S PLACE.
IT WAS A CLOSER THING THAN THEY WOULD HAVE YOU BELIEVE, THESE DAYS. IF NOT FOR BLOODRAVEN...
I'D ALWAYS HEARD THAT IT WAS BAELOR BREAKSPEAR WHO WON THE BATTLE. HIM AND PRINCE MAEKAR.
THE HAMMER AND THE ANVIL? THE SINGERS LEAVE OUT MUCH AND MORE.
"DAEMON WAS THE WARRIOR HIMSELF THAT DAY.
"NO MAN COULD STAND BEFORE HIM.
"HE BROKE LORD ARRYN'S VAN TO PIECES...
"...AND SLEW THE KNIGHT OF NINESTARS AND WILD WYL WAYNWOOD...

"...BEFORE COMING UP AGAINST SER GWAYNE CORBRAY OF THE KINGSGUARD.
"FOR NEAR AN HOUR THEY DANCED TOGETHER ON THEIR HORSES, WHEELING AND CIRCLING AND SLASHING AS MEN DIED ALL AROUND THEM.

"IT'S SAID THAT WHENEVER BLACKFYRE AND LADY FORLORN CLASHED, YOU COULD HEAR THE SOUND FOR A LEAGUE AROUND.
"IT WAS HALF A SONG AND HALF A SCREAM, THEY SAY.
"BUT WHEN AT LAST LADY FORLORN FALTERED, BLACKFYRE CLOVE THROUGH SER GWAYNE'S HELM AND LEFT HIM BLIND AND BLEEDING.
"DAEMON DISMOUNTED TO SEE THAT HIS FALLEN FOE WAS NOT TRAMPLED, AND COMMANDED REDTUSK TO CARRY HIM BACK TO THE MAESTERS IN THE REAR.
"AND THERE WAS HIS MORTAL ERROR...
"...FOR THE RAVEN'S TEETH HAD GAINED THE TOP OF WEEPING RIDGE, AND BLOODRAVEN SAW HIS HALF-BROTHER'S ROYAL STANDARD THREE HUNDRED YARDS AWAY, AND DAEMON AND HIS SONS BENEATH IT.

"HE SLEW AEGON FIRST, THE ELDER OF THE TWINS, FOR HE KNEW DAEMON WOULD NEVER LEAVE THE BOY WHILST WARMTH LINGERED IN HIS BODY, THOUGH WHITE SHAFTS FELL LIKE RAIN.
"NOR DID HE...

"...THOUGH SEVEN ARROWS PIERCED HIM, DRIVEN AS MUCH BY SORCERY AS BY BLOODRAVEN'S BOW.
"YOUNG AEMON TOOK UP BLACKFYRE WHEN THE BLADE SLIPPED FROM HIS DYING FATHER'S FINGERS...
"...SO BLOODRAVEN SLEW HIM TOO, THE YOUNGER OF THE TWINS.
"THUS PERISHED THE BLACK DRAGON AND HIS SONS.

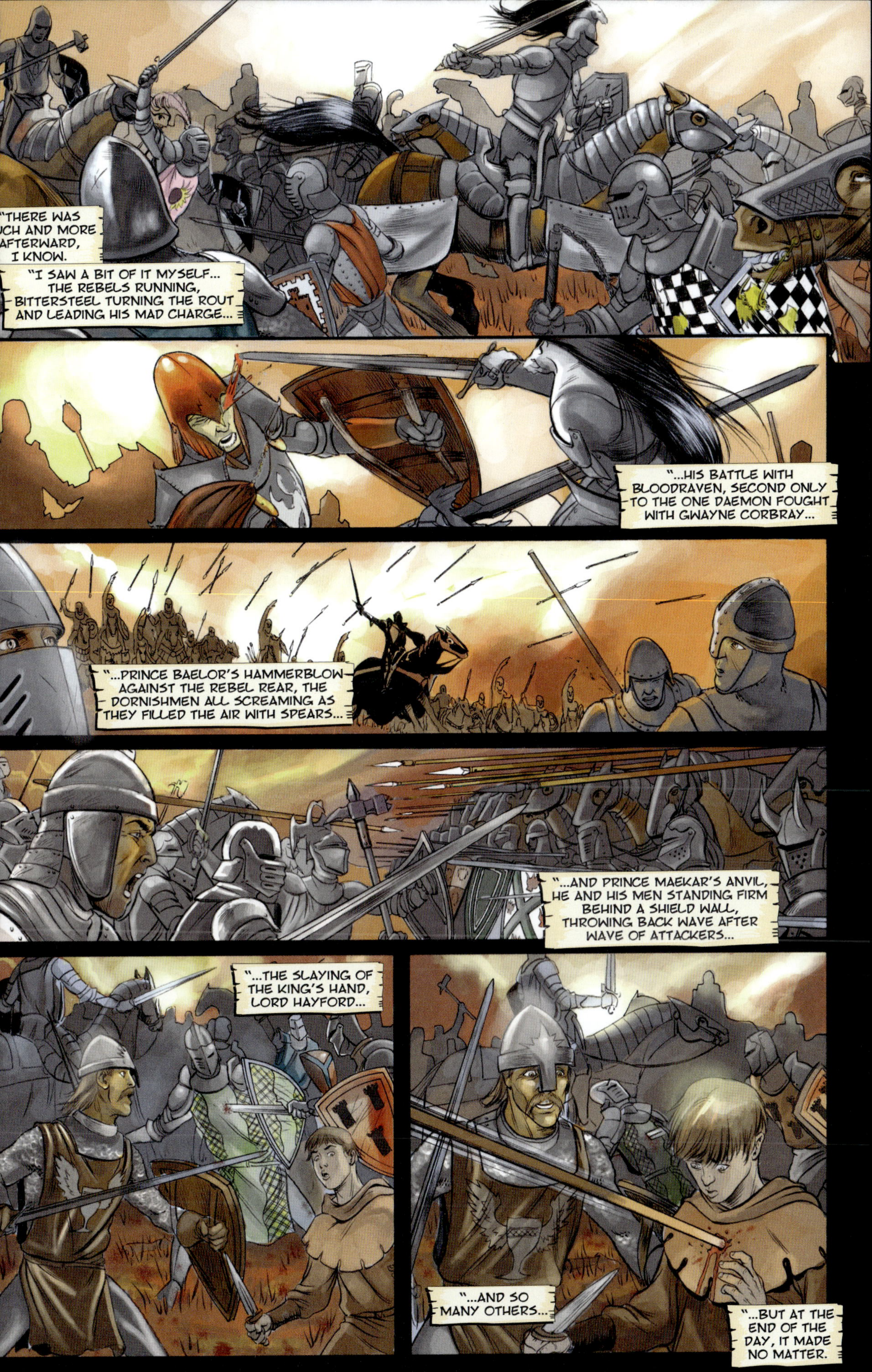
"THERE WAS ...UCH AND MORE AFTERWARD, I KNOW.
"I SAW A BIT OF IT MYSELF... THE REBELS RUNNING, BITTERSTEEL TURNING THE ROUT AND LEADING HIS MAD CHARGE...
"...HIS BATTLE WITH BLOODRAVEN, SECOND ONLY TO THE ONE DAEMON FOUGHT WITH GWAYNE CORBRAY...
"...PRINCE BAELOR'S HAMMERBLOW AGAINST THE REBEL REAR, THE DORNISHMEN ALL SCREAMING AS THEY FILLED THE AIR WITH SPEARS...
"...AND PRINCE MAEKAR'S ANVIL, HE AND HIS MEN STANDING FIRM BEHIND A SHIELD WALL, THROWING BACK WAVE AFTER WAVE OF ATTACKERS...
"...THE SLAYING OF THE KING'S HAND, LORD HAYFORD...
"...AND SO MANY OTHERS...
"...BUT AT THE END OF THE DAY, IT MADE NO MATTER.

"THE WAR WAS OVER WHEN DAEMON DIED.
"A GREAT BATTLE IS A TERRIBLE THING, BUT IN THE MIDST OF BLOOD AND CARNAGE, THERE IS SOMETIMES ALSO BEAUTY, BEAUTY THAT COULD BREAK YOUR HEART.
"I WILL NEVER FORGET THE WAY THE SUN LOOKED WHEN IT SET UPON THE REDGRASS FIELD...
"...TEN THOUSAND MEN HAD DIED, AND THE AIR WAS THICK WITH MOANS AND LAMENTATIONS, BUT ABOVE US THE SKY TURNED GOLD AND RED AND ORANGE, SO BEAUTIFUL IT MADE ME WEEP TO KNOW THAT MY SONS WOULD NEVER SEE IT.
"SO CLOSE A THING... IF DAEMON HAD RIDDEN OVER GWAYNE CORBRAY AND LEFT HIM HIS FATE, HE MIGHT HAVE BROKE MAEKAR'S LEFT BEFORE BLOODRAV COULD TAKE THE RIDGE. THE DAY WOULD HAVE BELONGED TO THE BLACK DRAGON THEN."
DAEMON MIGHT HAVE BEEN SITTING ON THE IRON THRONE BY THE TIME BAELOR COULD HAVE COME UP WITH HIS STORMLORDS AND HIS DORNISHMEN.
AND ROGER OF PENNYTREE MIGHT BE ALIVE TODAY. HE WOULD BE A KNIGHT SOMEPLACE, A TRUER KNIGHT THAN ME.
AND SER ARLAN WOULD HAVE HAD NO NEED FOR A GUTTER BORN LAD FROM FLEA BOTTOM. I MIGHT HAVE ENDED ON THE GALLOWS, OR BEEN SENT OFF TO THE NIGHT'S WATCH TO WALK THE WALL UNTIL I DIED...
THE SINGERS CAN GO ON ABOUT THEIR HAMMER AND THEIR ANVIL, SER, BUT IT WAS THE KINSLAYER WHO TURNED THE TIDE WITH A WHITE ARROW AND A BLACK SPELL.
MSW

MSM
11112003

WSM
12222003

BWS

BWS
BWS
COPY
COPY

Ser Baelor Targaryen
Prince of Dragonstone

Ser Maekar Targaryen
Prince of Summerhall

Ser Valarr Targaryen
Heir of Dragonstone

Ser Daeron Targaryen
Heir of Summerhall

Ser Willem Wylde

Ser Donnel
of Duskendale

Ser Roland Crakehall

Ser Aerion Targaryen
Prince Royal

Ser Damon Lannister
Lord of Casterly Rock

Ser Leo Tyrell
Lord of Highgarden

Ser Medgar Tully
Lord of Riverrun

Ser Gawen Swann
Lord of Stonehelm

Ser Pearce Caron
Lord of the Marches

Ser Lyonel Baratheon
Heir of Storm's End

Ser Tybolt Lannister
Heir of Casterly Rock

Ser Androw Ashford
Heir of Ashford

Ser Robert Ashford

Ser Humfrey Hardyng

Ser Robyn Rhysling
Ser Thurgood Fell
Ser Harys Graceford
Ser Raymun Fossoway
Ser Grance Morrigen
Ser Steffon Fossoway
Heir of Cider Hall
Ser Quentyn Tarth
Ser Benjamin Avery
Ser Michael Miller
Ser Michael Crowell
Ser William Tortoll
Ser Ernest Dabell
Ser Pascal Dabell
Ser Lester Dabell
Ser Raymond Rychard
Ser Walder of Woodmere
Ser Humfrey Beesbury
Ser Duncan the Tall

George R.R. Martin's The Hedge Knight

Set one hundred years before the events in George R.R. Martin's epic fantasy series, A Song of Ice and Fire, *The Hedge Knight* graphic novel chronicles a young squire as he travels the cruel and complex path to knighthood in the Seven Kingdoms.

Shouldering his fallen master's sword and shield, Duncan (or "Dunk") is determined to reinvent himself as a knight in a nearby tournament. But first Dunk needs a sponsor, and that requirement sends him down a road studded with friends, foes, adventure, and hidden agendas. One such friend is Egg, who becomes Dunk's squire, yet even he may hold secret motivations of his own.

In this gripping prequel, Dunk and Egg seek glory in a world both familiar and new to *Game of Thrones* fans. What the two fortune seekers encounter, however, is a world of distrust and political machinations. Chivalry is not lost while Dunk holds fast to his dreams of honor. But such outdated virtues make him a target—and they may even lead to his ruin. This vivid and elaborately wrought tale brings new dimension to George R. R. Martin's beloved world.

PARENTAL ADVISORY

ISBN-13: 978-1477849101
$18.99 US
51899
9 781477 849101

T+